160207

A PLACE APART

Houses of Christian Hospitality and Prayer in Europe

BELGIUM

FRANCE

DISCARD

St Patrick's Seminary & University
Library Collection
320 Middlefield Road
Menlo Park, CA 94025
www.stpatricksseminary.org

Janet L. Joy

RAPHAEL PUBLISHING
MILTON, WA

C0-DVG-179

BX
2438.5
.J663
2000

© Janet L. Joy 2000. All rights reserved.

Illustrations and text may not be reproduced in any form or by any means without the consent of the religious order that may hold copyright, and of the publisher.

Art work page 4, courtesy of Poor Clare Monastery, Belleville, IL; cover and page 120, courtesy of Poor Clare Monastery, Rosswell, NM; pages 28 and 120, courtesy of St. Teresa's Press, Flemington, NJ. Prayer of St. Colette, courtesy of Monastere Sainte-Claire, Poligny (Jura), France.

French translations by: Natalie Curtis
Cecile Schossow

Library of Congress Control Number: 00-090500

ISBN:0-9673074-6-5

St. Patrick's Seminary & University
Library Collection
320 Middlefield Road
Menlo Park, CA 94025
www.stpatricksseminary.org

RAPHAEL PUBLISHING
P. O. Box 750
Milton, WA 98354

Printed by Valley Press, Puyallup, WA

To my sister Connie
Woman of wisdom and grace
Tireless devotion to family
Source of peace and joy
Strength and guidance
Nurturing haven
Blessing for all.

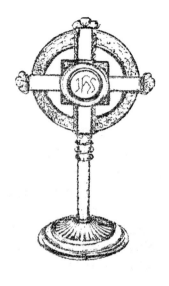

Blessed be
JESUS CHRIST
in
the Most
Holy Sacrament
of the altar!

INTRODUCTION

A PLACE APART – Belgium and France – is the last of seven small guidebooks that I have compiled over the past four years. It has truly been a labor of love!

The intrepid pilgrim will find food for thought among these one hundred and thirty nine listings, and can expect a most memorable experience from a time apart in any of these houses of Christian hospitality and prayer, for whatever length of stay.

This pertinent information will enable one to make an initial contact to explore future arrangements and to gather more extensive details. Each house is run differently, and upon request, will send a booking form and other literature that describes its programs, accommodations, and fees.

Feedback that I have received from travelers who have stayed in monasteries, convents, and the like has been very positive, and most have said it was one of the highlights of their trip.

I am grateful to all the religious groups who graciously accepted my invitation to be listed in this and all the European guidebooks. Their responses were warm and friendly, expressing a true love for God and for His children.

May St. Raphael the Archangel protect you and your loved ones on your spiritual journey. BON VOYAGE!

Janet L. Joy

BELGIUM

Abdij Affligem
Abdijstraat 6
1790 Affligem
Roman Catholic Benedictine

Tel: 053 66 70 25
Fax: 053 68 11 90
Contact: Guestmaster

Open To: Individuals, groups for Retreats, Conferences, and exhibitions in the Cultural Center.

Accommodation: Hospitality is provided in the Abbey Guest House in 15 bedrooms, meals included. Max. length of stay a few days. Lodging for youth groups possible in Reception Center (max. 60 persons), meals not included. Contact Brother in charge of youth groups.

Guests Admitted To: Abbey Church to join the monks for Mass and the Divine Office, sung in Dutch. Sunday Mass and Vespers in Latin Gregorian Chant. Grounds that are open to guests.

Of Interest: St. Peter and Paul Benedictine Abbey, founded in 1083, has a rich history that includes the founding or restoration of several other monasteries. It is a place of pilgrimage to Our Lady of Affligem, a devotion connected to a visit by St. Bernard of Clairvaux in 1146. The abbey was suppressed in 1796 by French revolutionaries, and monastic life was not restored until 1837 by six of the surviving monks in the town of Dendermonde. In 1870 a group of monks returned to the ruins. Today, among their many activities, the monks publish a periodical for liturgy, and they make fruit wine.

Access: Rail: Sta. Aalst (nearest town). Road: E40, exit 19A. Brussels 20 km.

Norbertijnenabdij Averbode   Tel: 013 780 440
Abdijstraat 1   Fax: 013 780 439
3271 Averbode   Contact: Guestmaster
Roman Catholic Norbertine

Open To: Individuals, groups for Retreats. Residential and day use. Spiritual Direction available.

Accommodation: Hospitality is provided in the Abbey Hotellerie for retreatants, full board.

Guests Admitted To: Abbey Church for liturgical services in Dutch and Latin Gregorian Chant. Guided Tours by prior arrangement in writing. Spring Concerts. Summer Art Exhibits. Gift/Book Shop.

Of Interest: The Abbey of Averbode was founded in 1134 by the Abbey of St. Michel of Antwerpen. The Regular Canons of the Order of Premontre have been a center of spiritual life, hospitality, and help to the poor, working closely with parishes and in cultural activities. Their life is based on the Gospel of Jesus Christ, the Rule of St. Augustine, and the ideals of St. Norbert.

Access: Rail: Zichem Sta. (or Testelt), Line 35 (Landen – Leuven – Aarschot – Hasselt). Road: A13/E313 (Antwerpen – Aachen), Exit 23 (Geel-West). A2/E314 (Leuven – Lummen – Aachen), Exit 23 (Tielt-Winge), or Exit 25 (Halen).

BANNEUX – La Vierge des Pauvres
Rue de l'Esplanade, 57
4141 Banneux Notre-Dame
Roman Catholic

Tel: 32 4 360 02 22
Fax: 32 4 360 82 39
Contact: Rector and
Pastoral Team

Open To: Pilgrims. An atmosphere of prayer and peace must be maintained with respect for the environment. Modest dress. May – October.

Accommodation: Centre d'Accueil de Chaityfontaine, Chaityfontaine, 8, 4860 Pepinster, Belgium. Tel: 32 4 360 91 71. Fax: 32 4 360 91 73.

Guests Admitted To: The Little Chapel for Mass. Blessing of the Sick. Rosary. The Spring (Source), 100 m. from the chapel. Audio-visual display (French).

Of Interest: Devotion to the Virgin of the Poor dates back to 1933 when Mary appeared to Mariette, the eldest child of the poor Beco family. The first of eight apparitions took place at the small garden in front of their house. During the second apparition, the child was led to the spring and instructed to put her hands in the water. Mary requested that a small chapel be built here during the fourth apparition, and it was built on the spot where she appeared. Our Lady entrusted the child with a secret on the sixth visit. The mosaic stones along the road leading to the spring mark the spots where Mariette dropped to her knees in prayer, despite the bitter cold. The Sanctuary welcomes large numbers of pilgrims, and it has grown into a shrine 'for all nations', as Mary wished it to be. Banneux Notre-Dame is a tiny hamlet in the District of Sprimont. It is situated on a plateau in the Ardenne Forest, between the beautiful valleys of Ambleve, Vesdre and Hoegne.

Access: Road: E40 east of Liege, then 24 km. on E25.

Abbey Notre Dame de Clairefontaine   Tel: 061 46 61 59
6830 Bouillon   061 46 74 24
Roman Catholic Cistercienne   Contact: Guest Sister

Open To: Individuals, groups for Retreats. Silence is encouraged.

Accommodation: Hospitality is provided in 20 guest rooms, meals included.

Guests Admitted To: Abbey Church to join the nuns for Mass and the Divine Office. Grounds that are open to guests.

Of Interest: The Cistercian Abbey of Notre-Dame de Clairefontaine is a place of solitude, peace and beauty. It is situated in a valley surrounded by forested land. The abbey was rebuilt in the 1930's, sixty kilometers from the ruins of the original abbey. The church was built in 1935.

Access: Road: E411 to Libramont, Exit 25 in direction of Reims-Sedan to Bouillon (30 km.). Bus at Libramont, Bertrix, Paliseul, Sedan (Fr.).

Monastere du Precieux Sang et de Notre-Dame du Mont Carmel
Schuttersstraat, 5   Tel: 050 34 36 42
8000 Brugge   Contact: Guest Sister
Roman Catholic Carmelite

Open To: Individuals for Retreats, or a time away in silence and peace. No tourists.

Accommodation: Hospitality is provided in the small Guest House in 7 single bedrooms, meals included.

Guests Admitted To: Chapel to join the nuns for Mass and the Divine Office. Small garden area.

Of Interest: Carmel of Brugge was founded in 1626, and there are several nationalities represented at the monastery. The monastery workshop creates lovely nativity scenes, both in wax and ceramic. The nuns make floral decorations, botanical note cards using pressed flowers, and have a pastry shop on the premises.

Access: Rail: Brugge Sta., then autobus, stop Sint-Jorisstraat. Trains from Brussels every half hour. Brugge approx. 88 km. NW of Brussels on canals connecting with Zeebrugge and Costende on the North Sea.

Monasterium de Wijngaard   Tel: 050 33 00 11
Oud-Begijnhof, 30   Fax: 050 33 18 81
8000 Brugge   Contact: Guest Sister
Roman Catholic Benedictine, The Daughters of the Church

Open To: Women, girls, married couples for a peaceful stay in an atmosphere of silence and serenity. Also, Days of Meditation, Conferences, Study Groups in the Diocesan Center for Liturgy and Pastoral Work.

Accommodation: Hospitality is provided in the Priory Guest House for a minimum of 3 days and nights. Also, residential possibilities for groups.

Guests Admitted To: Church to join the sisters for liturgical celebrations. Museum (former Beguine's house).

Of Interest: The Monastery of the Vineyard, founded in 1927, was formerly a Beguinage in the *13th c.* that provided a new kind of religious life for women. Today, Benedictine Sisters reside in the ancient buildings. A group of women called 'addicta' dedicate themselves to the same apostolic work in parishes, and are trained and supported by the monastery, though they do not necessarily live there.

Access: Good public transport.

Monastery of the Exaltation of the Cross
5590 Chevetogne
Latin and Byzantine Rite Catholic
Benedictine

Tel: 083 21 17 63
Fax: 083 21 60 45
Contact: Abbey
Guestmaster
House of Bethany
Guestmaster

Open To: Individuals, married couples, families, young people for rest and spiritual renewal. Study Weeks offered by Christians from various churches in the Lambert Beauduin Ecumenical Center.

Accommodation: Hospitality is provided in the abbey for men Meals taken with the monks. The House of Bethany accommodates other guests, with meals taken in the monastery. Max. stay 10 days.

Guests Admitted To: Latin Church. Oriental Church. Library. Iconography Workshop. Book Store. Grounds.

Of Interest: The Benedictine Monastery of the Exaltation of the Cross was founded in 1925 at Amay and relocated to Chevetogne in 1939. Its primary mission is to pray and work for the unity of Christians. The founder, Dom Lambert (1873 – 1960) was a pioneer of the ecumenical movement in the Catholic Church. As a center of prayer, the community celebrates at the same time the liturgies of the West and the Orthodox East, integrating into its life the spiritual treasures of the different churches, seeking to love them and make them known and loved by all.

Access: Rail: Sta. Ciney (Line Brussels-Luxembourg), then Bus 43 or taxi. Road: E411, Exit N21 (Houyet-Custinne) in direction of Chevetogne.

Abbaye de Maredsous   Tel: 082 69 82 11
5537 Denee   Fax: 082 69 83 21
E-mail:abbe@maredsous.be   Contact: Guestmaster
Roman Catholic Benedictine

Open To: Individuals, groups for Retreats, rest and renewal. Spiritual Direction available.

Accommodation: Hospitality is provided in the Hotellerie in several guest rooms, meals included.

Guests Admitted To: Monastery Church to join the community for Mass and the Divine Office, sung in French. Welcome Center. Library. Cafeteria. Gift Shop. Grounds.

Of Interest: The Abbey of Maredsous was founded in 1872, and is located in the Valley of Molignee. The monks run a school, printing press, record cassette tapes of the Sunday Divine Office, and operate a Bible and Computer Center. They make cheese, beer, ceramics, and wood crafts.

Access: Road: N96, Bus Line Namur-Maredsous, stops at the monastery. Dinant 20 km. Namur 30 km.

Monastere Notre-Dame   Tel: 071 72 00 48
Rue du Monastere, 1   Fax: 071 72 73 92
5644 Ermeton-sur-Biert   Contact: Soeur Hotelier
Roman Catholic Benedictine

Open To: Individuals, groups, married couples, families for Retreats, Conferences, Days of Reflection and Christian Formation, and sessions on Benedictine Spirituality.

Accommodation: Hospitality is provided in the Hotellerie in 28 bedrooms (5 for couples). Also, one self-catering cabin for families (7 persons).

Guests Admitted To: Monastery Church to join the sisters for liturgical services. Divine Office chanted in French. Chapel *(13ᵗʰ c.).* Castle. Library. Grounds.

Of Interest: The Monastery of Notre-Dame was founded in Bruxelles in 1917 and transferred to its present location in 1936. The sisters offer a wide variety of spiritual activities with opportunities for young people to dialogue in a Christian setting. Young women wishing to share in the monastic life of prayer and work are welcome year round and should contact the Prioress. The sisters do bookbinding, leatherwork, postcard design, and their handicrafts are sold at the monastery or by mail order.

Access: Road: E42, Exit Nr. 14 Sambreville, Fosses-la-Ville, Saint-Gerard, Ermeton-sur-Biert. RN36 (Dinant-Philippeville) Anthee, Ermeton-sur-Biert.

Abbaye Notre-Dame de Soleilmont
6220 Fleurus
Roman Catholic Cistercian

Open To: Individuals for Retreats. Public welcome to join the sisters for daily Mass and Vespers.

Accommodation: Hospitality is provided in the monastery's guest quarters for retreatants.

Guests Admitted To: Chapel. Grounds that are open to guests.

Of Interest: Since the *12ᵗʰ c.,* nuns have lived at Soleilmont. In 1963 a fire destroyed part of the ancient abbey, and the nuns settled nearby along the Cemetery of Charleroi. The Cistercian tradition is maintained in the new monastery built in a wooded area twenty years ago. Some families occupy the ruins of the old abbey.

Access: Road: South of Fleurus between Villers-la-Ville and Aulne.

Abdij der Norbertijnen Tel: 02 270 96 92
Kerkplein, 1 Contact: Guestmaster
1850 Grimbergen
Roman Catholic Norbertine Canons

Open To: Individuals, small groups for Retreats. Spiritual
Direction available. Youth groups June – October. Visitors
welcome for Guided Tours upon request. Public welcome for
church services, in Flemish.

Accommodation: Hospitality is provided in the monastery's
guest quarters for retreatants.

Guests Admitted To: Abbey Church *(17th c.)* to join the monks
for Mass and the Divine Office. Astronomical Observatory Mira,
located at Abdijstraat, 20 (persons over age 14), Sept. - June.
Meteorological Sta. Contact for current fees and schedule. Gift
Shop.

Of Interest: Grimbergen Abbey was founded in 1128 and is the
oldest Norbertine Abbey in Belgium that is still standing. The
Canons' life is woven around a daily rhythm of prayer as they
study theology, teach religion, run parishes, and host cultural
programs. There are many fine works of art in the church and
elsewhere in the monastery. A new building houses the
archives, library, and the monks' quarters.

Access: Rail: Sta. Brussels-North, then Bus 231 or for
Grimbergen-Humbeek. Road: The Ring, exit 7, and N202 or
A12 and N211. Located 12 km. north of Brussels.

St. Joseph's Sanctuary Tel: 016 22 42 38
St.-Antoniusberg, 7 Fax: 016 22 55 42
3000 Leuven
Roman Catholic Priests of the Sacred Hearts of Jesus and Mary

Open To: Pilgrims.

Accommodation: None on sanctuary grounds.

Guests Admitted To: Chapel.

Of Interest: The remains of Fr. Damien of Molokai, one of the newest saints in the Roman Catholic Church, are buried in the crypt at the Sanctuary. A lovely stained glass window depicts Damien and the lepers. Joseph de Veuster (1840-1889) was born in Tremelo, where one can visit the Fr. Damien House and Museum. In 1864 he went to Hawaii as a missionary, and to the Leper Colony on Molokai in 1873 where he was to spend the rest of his life, contracting the disease in 1885.

Access: Rail: Trains every half hour. Brussels 35 km. Leuven to Tremelo 20 km.

Abbaye de la Paix Notre-Dame
54, Boulevard d'Avroy
4000 Liege
Roman Catholic Benedictine

Tel: 32 4 223 77 20
Fax: 32 4 223 35 80
Contact: Guest Sister

Open To: Individuals for Retreats, or simply for rest and renewal in a place of peace and quiet.

Accommodation: Hospitality is provided in the abbey's guest rooms.

Guests Admitted To: Abbey Church (1690) to join the sisters for Mass and the Divine Office, sung in French. Grounds.

Of Interest: The Abbey of Our Lady of Peace was founded in 1627, and is the only Benedictine Monastery in Liege whose lifestyle has survived without interruption to this day. A boarding school was opened next to the monastery in 1797, and the present school continues the tradition. Other activities that the sisters engage in include lace making, painting on porcelain and silk, and baking cookies. Their goods are sold in the Gift Shop.

Access: Good public transport.

Monastere des Carmelites de Cornillon
Rue de Robermont, 2
4020 Liege   Contact: Prioress
Roman Catholic

Open To: Pilgrims/visitors are welcome for daily Mass, in
French, and sometimes in Gregorian Chant. From Easter to All
Saints Day, there is the possibility to join the nuns for Vespers
and Evening Prayer. Contact for current timetable.

Accommodation: None at the monastery.

Guests Admitted To: Chapel *(12th c.)*, maintained by the
Carmelites of Cornillon since 1860. Special Feast Day of
St. Juliana of Cornillon: August 7th.

Of Interest: St. Juliana (1191-1258) was inspired by our Lord
Jesus Christ over seven hundred and fifty years ago to compose
the Office for the Solemnity of Corpus Christi. As Prioress of
the Sisters of Cornillon, she suffered from trials and
persecutions, which forced her to seek refuge with some sisters
in Namur. She later came under the protection of Cistercian
Nuns, and is buried in the Cistercian Abbey of Villers-la-Ville.
A book on her life and the Feast of Corpus Christi is available
from Carmel of Cornillon.

Access: Rail: Liege Sta. (Guillemins), then Bus 1, 10 or 17.

Monastere Notre-Dame de Bethanie   Tel: ++ 32 50 38 31 71
Sijsen, 8   Fax: ++ 32 50 38 82 74
8210 Loppem Zedelgem   Contact: Guest Sister
Roman Catholic Benedictine
Congregation of the Queen of the Apostles

Open To: Individuals, groups for Retreats. Public welcome for church services.

Accommodation: Hospitality is provided for retreatants in several guest rooms.

Guests Admitted To: Monastery Church to join the sisters for Mass and the Divine Office, sung in Dutch. Grounds that are open to guests.

Of Interest: The Monastery of Our Lady of Bethanie was founded in 1921 by Dom Neve, Abbot of St. Andre of Bruges, to introduce monastic life to the young churches.

Access: Rail: SNCB Bruges, then Bus 66B in direction of Torhout or Roeselare, stop Vijverkasteel – 20 min. from monastery. Road: N32 or E40, Exit 7B Torhout. Bruges 7 km.

Monastere Sainte-Gertrude
Rue Haute, 58
1348 Louvain-la-Neuve
Roman Catholic Benedictine

Tel: **32 10 45 08 49
Contact: Sister in Charge

Open To: Individuals, married couples for a few days while on Retreat in silence. Opportunity for Spiritual Direction with an English-speaking sister.

Accommodation: Hospitality is provided in the Guest House for up to 10 persons. Max. stay 1 wk. Lunch and supper available in the community's dining room.

Guests Admitted To: Chapel to join the sisters for the Liturgy of the Hours.

Access: Road: E411 from Bruxelles, Exit 7; from Namur, Exit 9.

Monastere des Clarisses
'Clarte Notre-Dame'
Rue des Monasteres, 41
5020 Malonne
Roman Catholic Franciscan

Tel: 081 44 47 40
Contact: Guest Sister

Open To: Individuals, groups for Spiritual Retreats. Guests are encouraged to participate in liturgical services. Book by letter only.

Accommodation: Hospitality is provided in the Guest House Annex in 13 bedrooms. Meeting room for small groups. Library. Max. stay 10 days.

Guests Admitted To: Chapel to join the nuns for Mass and the Divine Office.

20

Of Interest: This Poor Clare Monastery was founded in 1903 by Monastere des Clarisses de Saint-Omer, Pas-de-Calais, France. It is situated in a beautiful area of rolling hills and lovely grounds for quiet walks. Guests are invited to spend a few hours doing yard work and gardening with the nuns in silence.

Access: Rail: Namur Sta., then bus to Malonne. Road: N22 and N51. Located 7 km. SW of Namur.

Norbertijnenabdij Postel
'Kontaktcentrum'
Abdijlaan, 16
2400 Mol
Roman Catholic Norbertine Fathers
Regular Canons of Premontre

Tel: 014 37 81 21
Fax: 014 37 81 23
Contact: Guestmaster

Open To: Individuals, Christian groups, including youth, for Retreats. Public welcome for church services. Guided Tour upon request. Contact: The Circle of the Guides of Mol, Frissehoeken, 48, 2400 Mol, Belgium. Tel: 014 31 45 95.

Accommodation: Hospitality is provided for retreatants.

Guests Admitted To: Abbey Church for liturgical services.

Of Interest: The Norbertine Abbey of Postel was founded in 1140 from the Norbertine Abbey, Floreffe, Belgium, In 1797, forces of the French Revolution confiscated all abbey properties and the Canons and lay brothers were dispersed. In 1847, the last surviving Norbertine of Postel returned with followers. The Canons and lay brothers engage in many apostolic works as well as material and cultural tasks such as dairy farming, environmental concerns, and art and culture, evident in library wing.

Access: Road: E34. Mol is 48 km. east of Antwerp.

Centre Spirituel 'La Pairelle' Tel: 081 46 81 11
Rue Lecomte, 25 Fax: 081 46 81 52
5100 Namur-Wepion Contact: Director
Roman Catholic Jesuit

Open To: Individuals, couples, families, groups for Retreats and other spiritual activities. Spiritual Direction available. Reservations in writing.

Accommodation: Hospitality is provided in the Retreat Center in several single and double bedrooms. Bathrooms each floor. Conference rooms, meeting rooms.

Guests Admitted To: Chapel. Library. Grounds.

Of Interest: 'La Pairelle' was established in 1971. The Jesuit Fathers and lay men and women organize retreats and are available to meet the spiritual needs of participants. Also, the Community of Bethanie is a group of young people who make a year's commitment to welcome persons in their age group.

Access: Rail: Sta. Namur, then 5 km. by taxi. By bus, stop E across from Namur Sta., then Bus 1 or 4. Stop at 'La Pairelle', then a 15-min. walk to the center. Road: N92 from Dinant.

Abbaye Notre-Dame de St.-Remy ASBL
5580 Rochefort Tel: 00 32 0 84 220 140
Roman Catholic Trappist Contact: Guestmaster

Open To: Men for Spiritual Retreats. Climate of silence must be respected. Spiritual Direction available.

Accommodation: Hospitality is provided in the Hotellerie in 14 rooms within the monastic cloister.

Guests Admitted To: Abbey Church to join the monks for Mass and the Divine Office, in French and Latin, sung in Gregorian Chant. Adoration of the Blessed Sacrament.

Of Interest: The Abbey of Our Lady of St. Remy was originally founded in 1230 by Cistercian Nuns. Monks took up residence in 1464. Monastic life ceased as a result of the French Revolution, but resumed in 1884. The monks engage in many activities, including the operation of a brewery.

Access: Rail: SNCB Jemelle Sta., then 4 km. by bus to Rochefort. Road: 12 km. east of Freeway E11 via N911.

Carmel de Rochefort
12, Avenue du Rond Point
5580 Rochefort
Roman Catholic Carmelite

Tel: 084 21 12 72 (0830 1100)
Contact: Mother Prioress

Open To: Women for Retreats, or simply a quiet place to stay while on pilgrimage.

Accommodation: Hospitality is provided in 4 bedrooms in Our Lady of Solitude Guest House. Ten rooms are also available nearby in another hospitality house, Tabeel, run by the nuns.

Guests Admitted To: House Chapel to join the nuns for daily Mass and the Divine Office.

Of Interest: Carmel of Rochefort was founded in 1906 and is situated close to the Marian Sanctuary of Beauraing.

Access: Road: 24 km. SE of Dinant.

How little known is the merciful love of Jesus! St. Therese

Zusters Clarissen   Tel: 03 568 75 57
Oud Broek, 8   Contact: Guest Sister
2960 Stabroek
Roman Catholic Franciscan

Open To: Individuals seeking Christian hospitality in an
atmosphere of peace and friendship.

Accommodation: Hospitality is provided in the convent in 5
guest rooms on the second floor (elevator). Shared bathroom.
Meals taken in common separate from the nuns. Guests may
help with various tasks as desired.

Guests Admitted To: Chapel to join the nuns for liturgical
services. Grounds.

Of Interest: The Convent of Poor Clare Nuns is situated in a
rural municipality of Antwerp in a beautiful forest that is ideal
for taking long, quiet walks among varying landscapes.
Approximately twenty five years ago the community moved
from their older, more traditional monastery to a more modern
living situation, yet they retain their contemplative point of
view.

Access: Road: Bus 65 from Antwerp to the end station Putte (50
min.), then 15 min. on foot to the convent.

Les Beatitudes | Tel: 00 32 71 61 12 68
Marie Mediatrice de Toutes Graces | Fax: 00 32 71 61 13 93
10, rue du Fourneau | Contact: Secretary
5651 Thy-le-Chateau
Roman Catholic

Open To: Individuals, groups for House Retreats, Days of Prayer and Recollection in silence. Schedule sent upon request. Reservations booked by letter only.

Accommodation: Hospitality is provided in one and two-bedded rooms. Shared showers/baths. Linens extra. Dining room, meeting rooms.

Guests Admitted To: Chapel to join the community for Eucharist and the Divine Office. Adoration of the Blessed Sacrament. Grounds.

Of Interest: The Community of the Beatitudes is primarily a contemplative community, founded in 1973 by a lay couple, Ephraim and Jo Croissant. It consists of priests, religious, and lay persons who pattern their lives on the example of the early Christians. One of their primary charisms is retreat work. There are approximately seventy houses worldwide, the majority in France and Europe.

Access: Rail: At Charleroi, take Line Walcourt-Couvin to Berzee. Call the house for pickup at the station. Road: N5 in direction of Gourdinne. Located halfway between Charleroi and Philippeville. Brussels 70 km.

Maison D'Accueil | Tel: 069 85 94 11
Place 6 | Contact: Secretary
7760 Velaines (Celles)
Roman Catholic Oblate Missionaries of Mary

Open To: Groups who bring their own program for Retreats, Conferences, Courses. Also for those who simply desire a restful time apart in a spiritual setting.

Accommodation: Hospitality is provided in 3 buildings in single and two-bedded rooms (max. 90 persons). Sink in each room, showers on ground floor. Cafeteria with set meal times. Conference rooms, meeting rooms, TV room, recreation room. The Fathers welcome an advance visit to learn of the various options. Complete information sent upon request.

Guests Admitted To: Chapel. Park-like grounds.

Of Interest: Maison D'Accueil, Maison Saint-Joseph, and Maison de Campeurs (hostel) are situated in an agricultural area, surrounded by woods and meadows in the village of Velaines. The city of Tournai is nearby and offers a wide range of cultural and sports activities.

Access: Road: Renaix 13 km., Leuze 17 km., Courtrai 40 km., Lille 40 km., Mons 50 km., Bruxelles 80 km.

Zusters Karmelietessen
Marshofstraat, 6
8908 Vlamertinge
Roman Catholic Carmelite

Open To: Pilgrims, especially during May and summer months.

Accommodation: None at the convent.

Guests Admitted To: Chapel of Our Lady Vrouw van Frezenberg.

Of Interest: A visit to this chapel of the Carmelite Nuns is the focus of many pilgrimages to the miraculous statue of the Blessed Virgin Mary, which was fully restored, with Spanish cloths, over ten years ago. The convent is a small castle that was bequeathed to the nuns by a benefactor following WWII. It is situated near the village of Ieper near many wartime cemeteries.

Access: Road: The road to Ieper.

Notre-Dame de Fichermont
Chemin de la Croix, 21
1410 Waterloo
Roman Catholic

Tel: 2 384 23 38
Fax: 2 387 28 38
Contact: Retreat
Secretary

Open To: Individuals, groups for Spiritual Retreats. Program information sent upon request.

Accommodation: Hospitality is provided in the Retreat House. Also, overnight facilities as space available.

Guests Admitted To: Chapel. Grounds.

Of Interest: The Community Le Verbe de Vie is a continuation of the mission of the Dominican Sisters who have served and ministered here for seventy five years.

Access: Rail: Sta. Brussels-Midi. Take Line Brussels-Charleroi (124) to Braine l'Alleud, then Bus Wavre at train sta. to Monument Gordon (look for monastery). Road: E19 (Paris – Mons – Nivelles). Past Nivelles, Circle Est, Exit 'Butte du Lion' in direction of Charleroi, N5. From Liege, E42, direction of Namur. At Daussoulx, E411, Exit Louvain La Neuve.

Abdij O. L. Vrouw van het H. Hart   Tel: 03 312 92 00
2390 Westmalle   Fax: 03 312 92 00
Roman Catholic Cistercienzer   Contact: Guestmaster

Open To: Men for Private Retreats. Also, for men discerning a call to monastic life. Spiritual Direction available. Guests are encouraged to participate in liturgical services. Public welcome for church services.

Accommodation: Hospitality is provided in the Abbey Guest House for a limited number of men at one time. Meals taken in guest house refectory.

Guests Admitted To: Abbey Church to join the monks for daily Mass and the Divine Office, chanted in Dutch. Library.

Of Interest: The Cistercian Abbey of the Sacred Heart of Mary was founded in 1794, and elevated to the status of Abbey in 1836. The monks are engaged in many activities including cheese-making, and they operate a brewery. The cheese is sold on weekdays at the gate of the abbey.

Access: Road: N12. Bus 41 (Antwerpen-Turnhout) stopdienst. Located 23 km. NE of Antwerp.

God of peace,

Gift of peace

Be our peace
and our joy

Let nothing trouble thee
Let nothing frighten thee
All things pass away ✠✠
God never changes ✠
Patience obtains all things
Nothing is wanting to him
who possesses God
God alone suffices ✠

St. Teresa's Bookmark

✠

FRANCE

Abbaye de Puyperoux   Contact: Guest Sister
16190 Aignes et Puyperoux
Roman Catholic
Soeur de la Sainte-Famille de Bordeaux

Open To: Individuals, groups for Retreats for persons seeking to spend a few days of silence in prayer and contemplation in a peaceful environment.

Accommodation: Hospitality is provided in the House of the Holy Family in single and double bedrooms. Dining room, meeting rooms.

Guests Admitted To: Chapel to join the sisters for liturgical services. Grounds.

Access: Road: 674 from Montmoreau or Angouleme, Exit D54 (Puyperoux). Angouleme 27 km.

Monastere du Carmel
2, pl. Marguerite-de-Lorraine
61000 Alencon
Roman Catholic Carmelite

Open To: Young women who are discerning a call to monastic life as a Carmelite Nun. Public welcome for Mass.

Accommodation: Hospitality is provided in the Guest House, an ancient manor built at the end of the *15th c.*

Guests Admitted To: Extern Chapel (1939) to join the nuns for Mass. Small room outside the cloister where a wax manger scenes may be viewed. These Nativity sets are sold here, along with religious articles and honey. Annual Exposition Sale first weekend of December.

Of Interest: Carmel of Alencon was founded in 1780. It is dedicated to the Sacred Heart of Jesus and the Immaculate Conception. The nuns promote devotion to Jesus by creating Nativity sets from wax. These may be mail ordered, and information will be sent upon request. Some ruins of the ancient city still stand within the cloister, which is closed to the public. Alencon is the birthplace of St. Therese of the Child Jesus.

Access: Road: Le Mans 44.8 km.

Abbaye Notre-Dame de Vive-Fontaine Tel: 03 26 52 80 30
51270 Andecy Fax: 03 26 52 36 77
Roman Catholic Contact: Retreat
Community du Verbe de Vie Secretary

Open To: Individuals, groups, couples, families for Retreats, Courses, and other spiritual activities. Also, a year's Sabbatical available. Contact for further information.

Accommodation: Hospitality is provided in the abbey's guest quarters in single, double and triple-bedded rooms. When full, local hotel may be contacted.

Guests Admitted To: Chapel. Grounds.

Of Interest: The Community du Verbe de Vie is supported by brothers and sisters in Christ who gather together to celebrate the Lord, to pray for the Church, and to listen to the Word of God. Guests participate in the work of the community for one hour each day.

Access: Road: From Paris, A4 (Metz-Nancy), Exit La Ferte-sous-Jouarre in direction of Chalons-sur-Marne (D407) to Champaubert for Andecy. Turn right on D51. Andecy 2 km. from Baye.

Monastere des Bernardines
64600 Anglet
Roman Catholic 'Bernardines'
Servants of Mary

Tel: 59 63 84 34
Contact: Guest Sister

Open To: Women, young ladies for Silent Retreat.

Accommodation: Hospitality is provided in the monastery's guest rooms for 5 retreatants (max. stay 8 days). Meals taken with the community.

Guests Admitted To: Chapel to join the sisters for Mass and the Divine Office in French. Gift Shop. Grounds.

Of Interest: The Congregation of the Servants of Mary was founded by Fr. Louis Edward Cestac (1801-1868). In 1839, fourteen young penitents came to live at Notre-Dame du Refuge with their young mistress. Formerly known as Chateauneuf, it is situated among sandy hills, pine forests, and pastureland between Bayonne and Biarritz near the sea and the Spanish border. These were the first sisters to take religious vows in 1842 as the Servants of Mary. The Bernardines are a branch of the congregation but live a life of silence, solitude and prayer at their monastery on the grounds of the Mother House. Among their varied duties, they bind books, embroider, make liturgical ornaments and greeting cards, and garden.

Access: Road: N10. 3 km. south of Bayonne.

Abbaye St.-Etienne
19190 Aubazine
Roman Catholic
Community du Verbe de Vie

Tel: 05 55 84 61 12
Fax: 05 55 84 63 07
Contact: Retreat Secretary

Open To: Individuals for Retreats, Courses, Sabbaticals. Contact for further information.

Accommodation: Hospitality is provided in the abbey's guest quarters in single, double and triple-bedded rooms.

Guests Admitted To: Abbey Church. Grounds.

Of Interest: The Abbey of St. Stephen was founded in the 12th c. In 1986 it formed the Community du Verbe de Vie. Among the many courses at this Catholic School of Spirituality is the School of Prayer, rooted in the Liturgy and Daily Office, with special emphasis on the Eucharist celebration and Adoration of the Blessed Sacrament.

Access: Rail: Brive Sta. (Paris-Toulouse or Bordeaux-Lyon Lines). Then change trains for Aubazine Sta. (Line Brive-Tulle). Road: RN89. Brive 12 km. Tulle 18 km.

Monastere de la Theophanie
Le Ladeix
Route de Tulle
19190 Aubazine
Greek Melkite Catholic
Moniales de la Resurrection

Tel: 05 55 25 75 67
Contact: Superior

Open To: Individuals, groups, married couples, families seeking Christian hospitality in a monastic setting. Possibility to study icon painting, Eastern Catholic and Orthodox spirituality, and Greek and Arabic Church music. English spoken by some of the nuns.

Accommodation: Hospitality is provided in the Guest House in 10 single bedrooms. Two double rooms have private baths. Community showers.

Guests Admitted To: Monastery Church for the Divine Liturgy and Office in the Byzantine Rite, sung in French to Greek and Arabic melodies.

Of Interest: The Monastery of the Theophany houses a small community of Byzantine Catholic Nuns. Situated in a farmhouse, a former dependence of the Cistercian Abbey *(12th c.),* it is surrounded by about forty acres of woods and pastureland. The ancient abbey, a ten-minute walk away, is presently inhabited by a charismatic community. Guests may visit the abbey and the ruins of the priory. Monastere de la Theophanie sets in the foothills of the Massif Central Mountain Range, and is on the main road to Santiago de Compostela, the Shrine of St. James the Apostle in Spain. The church, a former barn, is covered with frescoes of the purest Greek style, and is considered to be a jewel of Byzantine art in France.

Access: Air: Paris-Brive Airport, then bus or taxi.
Rail: Paris-Toulouse to Brive La Gaillarde, then train or bus to Aubazine Sta. Call beforehand for pick-up. Sta. 4 km. from village, all uphill. Road: RN20 from Paris and Limoges or Cahors, then RN89, Exit Aubazine.

Abbaye de Bassac   Tel: 05 45 81 94 22
16120 Bassac   Fax: 05 45 81 98 41
Roman Catholic   Contact: Guestmaster
Freres Missionnaires de Sainte-Therese

Open To: Individuals for Private Retreats (max. stay 8 days). Groups for Retreats, other spiritual activities, cultural events.

Accommodation: Hospitality is provided in 40 bedrooms, each with sink. Bathrooms/showers each floor. Conference and meeting rooms.

Guests Admitted To: Abbey Church. Chapel of Sainte-Therese of the Child Jesus. Park-like grounds for quiet walks along the Charente River. Guided Tours available.

Of Interest: Abbaye de Bassac was founded in 1003. Its history of pilgrimage dates back to the Crusades when the monastery received one of the cords used to bind Jesus Christ to the pillar of flagellation. The monks also had in their possession one of

the Blessed Virgin Mary's belts. These relics were destroyed
during the Religious War of 1562. The abbey was abandoned
during the French Revolution, and monastic life did not resume
until 1947 with the arrival of the present fathers and brothers.
A pilgrimage in honor of their patron saint, Therese, is
celebrated every year at the end of September or early in
October.

Access: Rail: Jarnac Sta., then taxi 7 km.

Prieure Sainte-Marie   Tel: 02 43 66 43 66
La Cotellerie   Fax: 02 43 66 43 67
53170 Bazougers   Contact: Fathers and Brothers
Roman Catholic
Petits-Freres de Marie, Mere du Redempteur

Open To: Individuals, groups, families for Spiritual Retreats,
rest and renewal. English, French, German and Italian spoken.

Accommodation: Hospitality is provided in the Hotellerie in
15 bedrooms (26 beds). Also, the Youth Hotellerie has 2
dormitories (19 and 30 beds). Conference rooms, workshop
rooms. Length of stay 1 – 10 days.

Guests Admitted To: Canoniale Church 'St. Mary, Mother of
the Redeemer' (1994) to join the community for Mass and Office,
chanted in French. Crypt, dedicated to the Martyrs of Laval
(+1794). Religious library. Audio-visual presentation.

Of Interest: Les Chanoines Reguliers de Marie, Mere du
Redempteur, founded in 1971, follow the Rule of St. Augustine.
They combine community life, prayer and preaching with a
special emphasis on the Eucharist and devotion to Mary.
Homemade products are sold in the Gift Shop such as honey,
fruit bars, bonbons, nougat, cookies, cider and apple juice. They
also sell other religious articles.

Access: Rail: SNCF (TGV Atlantique) to Laval, then taxi to the
Priory. Road: D21. Laval 15 km.

Abbaye de Bellefontaine
49122 Begrolles en Mauges
Roman Catholic Cistercian

Tel/Fax: 02 41 75 60 46
Contact: Pere Hotelier

Open To: Individuals, groups for Retreats. Spiritual Direction available. French spoken. Advance reservations required.

Accommodation: Hospitality is provided in 50 single, 15 double bedrooms, sink in each room. Showers/bathrooms each floor. Conference rooms, dining room, oratory. Elevator.

Guests Admitted To: Abbey Church to join the monks for Mass and the Divine Office in French. Chapel of Notre-Dame de Bon Secours. Audio-visual presentation on monastery life. Library. Gift Shop – products from the monastery gardens and other monasteries. Mail-order available.

Of Interest: The Abbey of Bellefontaine was originally founded in 1100 and has been a Benedictine Abbey from its beginnings. The monks were forced into exile during the French Revolution. In 1816 the Trappist monks returned from America and purchased the remainder of the property. Many buildings date back to the end of the *19th c.* One wing was built in 1960. The faithful have come here on pilgrimage for hundreds of years on August 15th, the Feast Day of Our Lady of Bon Secours, to the chapel near the monastery. The *13th c.* statue of Notre-Dame de Bellefontaine may be viewed in the church.

Access: Rail: Sta. Cholet, then 13 km. Road: N752 north of Cholet. Nantes 56 km. Angers 58 km.

Abbaye Sainte-Marie du Desert   Tel: 05 61 85 61 32
31530 Bellegarde Sainte-Marie   Fax: 05 61 85 04 32
Roman Catholic Cistercian   Contact: Guestmaster

Open To: Individuals, groups for Retreats, Days of Recollection, Pilgrimage. Advance reservations suggested. Max. stay 8 days.

Accommodation: Hospitality is provided in the guest quarters of the Conventual Building in 25 bedrooms. Dining room, conference rooms. Only an overnight stay for pilgrims.

Guests Admitted To: Abbey Church to join the monks for Mass and the Divine Office. Pilgrimage Chapel. Reception Court. Monastery Shop (honey, candy, toiletries, and other homemade and handcrafted articles). Annual pilgrimage for the Nativity of Notre-Dame: First Sunday in Sept., or Sept. 8th if on a Sunday.

Of Interest: Abbaye Sainte-Marie du Desert was founded in 1852 from Abbaye Notre-Dame d'Aiguebelle. All the brothers helped build the abbey and monastic life flourished. The architectural plan is Cistercian, expressing an austere beauty. The walls are of a natural finish, without adornment, and the rugged buildings are well-constructed in a Roman-Gothic style. The abbey is situated on one hundred and thirty hectares, and the monks grow a variety of grains as well as other crops. They co-exist in perfect communion with the resident deer population.

Access: Rail: Line Toulouse-Auch to Sta. Merenvielle or l'Isle-Jourdain, then Bus Semvat or taxi 15 km. Road: N124 and D24 from Toulouse. D1 from Colomiers, Levignac, Le Castera.

Chartreuse de Portes   Tel: 04 74 36 72 88
01470 Benonces   Fax: 04 74 36 11 15
Roman Catholic Carthusian   Contact: Prior

Open To: Visitors wishing to join the monks for Sunday Mass. The atmosphere of prayer and silence that this order has maintained for 900 years must be respected. Parents of the monks. Candidates discerning a vocation to Carthusian monastic life may spend time with the monks, sharing their life of prayer and work.

Accommodation: Hospitality is provided for overnight visits twice a year for parents of the monks.

Guests Admitted To: Monastery Church.

Of Interest: Chartreuse de Portes was founded in 1115 from the Grande Chartreuse, Saint-Pierre-de-Chartreuse, France, and construction began in 1125. St. Anthelme arrived in 1136 and became Prior of the Grande Chartreuse in 1139. The monastery was restored in 1640. In the 18th c., the monks were dispersed as a result of the French Revolution. They returned in 1855 and restored the monastery, but were once more dispersed in 1901 by the government. The property fell into the hands of different proprietors during the ensuing years and was allowed to deteriorate. The Carthusian Order repurchased the property in 1959, and the complex was completely restored by 1971. The monks' cells surround the cloister and cemetery where the remains of eight hundred monks are at rest. The monks of Chartreuse de Portes live a purely contemplative life, partly solitary, partly in community. Their duties include book-binding, woodworking, and forestry work. The monastery is situated in the Mountains of Bugey.

Access: Rail: Sta. Amberieu-en-Bugey (25 km.) or Sta. Tenay-Hauteville, then by car. Located 7 km. from the village. No public transportation to Chartreux.

Maison Saint-Conrad   Tel: 03 87 96 06 12
2, rue des Capucins   Fax: 03 87 96 14 31
57230 Bitche   Contact: Directress
Roman Catholic Secular Franciscan Order

Open To: Individuals, groups for Retreats, Conferences,
Seminars, Days of Recollection, Sacramental Preparation, and
for a time of rest and renewal. Possibility to meet with a
Capuchin priest. French, Italian and German spoken.

Accommodation: Hospitality is provided in the House of
St. Conrad in 28 bedrooms (24 are two-bedded). Also, dormitory
with 9 beds. Meeting rooms, 2 dining rooms.

Guests Admitted To: House Chapel to join the community for
daily prayer. Vespers at 17:15. Adoration of the Blessed
Sacrament. Garden.

Of Interest: Maison Saint-Conrad was originally part of the
ancient College of St. Augustine, and has been under the
management of the Capuchin branch of the Franciscan Order
since 1936. In 1960 the house underwent extensive remodeling
to adapt it for an enlarged ministry by the Capuchin Fathers
and Brothers and the Franciscan Missionary Sisters of Notre
Dame. The Secular Fraternity of St. Francis of Assisi has
operated the spirituality center since 1994. The house is
situated in the center of Bitche in the Regional Park of Vosgs,
and there is a beautiful promenade nearby. St. Conrad was a
Capuchin Brother at the Convent of Altotting in Germany from
1818 – 1894, and was gatekeeper for many years. He was
beautified in 1930 and canonized in 1934.

Access: Rail: To Metz Forbach or Strasbourg, then by taxi.
Road: Metz – Forbach – A34, Sarreguemines – N60, Strasbourg
– A34. Exit Haguenau. Follow signs for Schweighouse,
Niederbronn, Bitche. Sarreguemines 35 km. Strasbourg 80 km.
Metz 90 km.

Chartreuse de Selignac   Tel/Fax: 04 74 51 70 79
Simandre-Sur-Suran
01250 Ceyzeriat
Roman Catholic Carthusian Order

Open To: Young men interested in a vocation to this eremitic life may come for retreat, to live and work with the monks. Families of the monks may visit twice a year.

Accommodation: Hospitality is provided for young men in cells like those of the monks. Family members stay in the Hotellerie.

Guests Admitted To: Monastery Church to join the monks for Mass, Matins and Vespers, sung in Gregorian Chant.

Of Interest: Chartreuse of Selignac was founded in 1202 by an aristocrat from Coligny who fought in the Crusades. It is situated in the beautiful Valley of Revermont beneath the western ridge of the Jura Mountains. The monastery flourished, especially during the *15th c.,* but suffered ruin during the Thirty-Years War. Later it was restored and enjoyed new prosperity. The French Revolution interrupted life, and part of the monastery was destroyed. The monks repurchased the property in 1866, but in 1901 it fell to hard times. They returned in 1929 with the aid of a benefactor. The monks live a life of solitude in prayer and meditation. Their hermitages surround the main buildings. They perform manual labor and engage in intellectual pursuits, aided by a richly endowed library.

Access: Rail: SNCF: Simandre Sta., then 5 km.
Road: Oyonnax. Bourg-en-Bresse 20 km.

'Nazareth' Spirituality Center   Tel: 04 75 59 00 05
26120 Chabeuil   Fax: 04 75 59 17 96
Roman Catholic   Contact: Secretary
Cooperateurs Parroisiaux du Christ Roi

Open To: Individuals, couples, groups for Ignatian Retreats and other spiritual activities.

Accommodation: Hospitality is provided in the center in 60 bedrooms (10 are double). Conference rooms, large garden.

Guests Admitted To: Chapel. Grounds.

Of Interest: 'Nazareth', a house of spiritual formation and prayer, was originally an old textile factory that was converted into a residence for religious in 1934. It has been remodeled by the parish of Christ the King to be used mostly for retreats, encouraging men to evangelize in their parishes and in society. It is situated in the Rhone Valley at the foot of Mt. Vercors in the Drome Region of southeast France.

Access: Rail: Sta. Valence, then 9 km. Road: Paris-Marseille.

Monastere des Clarisses   Tel: 04 73 37 73 11
11, avenue de Villars   Fax: 04 73 31 18 65
63400 Chamalieres   Contact: Guest Sister
Roman Catholic Franciscan

Open To: Individuals for Retreats. Spiritual Direction available.

Accommodation: Hospitality is provided in the monastery's guest quarters in 7 bedrooms. Shared bathrooms. Conference room. Max. stay 8 days.

Guests Admitted To: Chapel to join the sisters for Mass and the Divine Office. Grounds.

Of Interest: The history of these Poor Clares dates back to 1535 when the Clarisses-Capucines Order was reformed, with the approval of Pope Paul III. In 1930 the Poor Clare Monastery of Lorgues transferred to its present location at Chamalieres. The sisters live a life of praise and prayer, work and fraternal life. Baking Eucharist wafers is a major work of the monastery.

Access: Rail: Sta. Clermont-Ferrand or Sta. Royat, then by bus. Road: Located west of Clermont-Ferrand.

Foyer de Charite
85, rue Geoffroy de Moirans
B.P. 11
26330 Chateauneuf-de-Galaure
Roman Catholic

Tel: 04 75 68 79 00
Fax: 04 75 68 66 91
Contact: Father of the Foyer

Open To: Individuals, groups for Six-Day Retreats in silence.

Accommodation: Hospitality is provided in the retreat house.

Guests Admitted To: House Chapel to join the community for Mass, morning and evening prayer, rosary. Adoration of the Blessed Sacrament. Grounds.

Of Interest: In 1936 Fr. Georges Finet, on the initiative of Marthe Robin, founded this Foyer, the first of many that are located around the world. Their main mission is the formation of lay people through fundamental retreats. Retreatants are inspired to go forth bringing the Good News to the world.

Access: Road: Chateauneuf de Galaure in Drome, approx. 80 km. south of Lyon.

Monastere Notre-Dame-de-Triors   Tel: 04 75 71 43 39
B. P. 1   Contact: Guestmaster
26750 Chatillon-Saint-Jean
Roman Catholic Benedictine

Open To: Men for Retreats, or a quiet time apart for prayer, rest and renewal. Limited facilities for women and families. Spiritual Direction available.

Accommodation: Hospitality is provided for men in the monastery. Meals taken with the monks in the refectory. Self-catering facilities for others in the guest houses.

Guests Admitted To: Monastery Church to join the monks for Mass and the Divine Office. Gift Shop (handicrafts by the monks – pottery, woolens, religious articles, homemade candies, as well as books, and recordings of Gregorian Chant). Grounds that are open to guests.

Of Interest: The Monastery of Our Lady of Triors was founded in 1984. It is situated in the foothills of the Alps. Monastic life revolves around a daily rhythm of prayer and work, with periods of silence and study.

Access: Road: A49 from Grenoble or Valence. Exit in direction of Bourg de Peage and Romans to D538. At Peyrins, take a right onto D69 in direction of Genissieux, then left before Chatillon-St.-Jean and follow signs to monastery.

Abbaye Notre-Dame de la Grace-Dieu
25530 Chaux Les Passavant   Tel: 03 81 60 44 45
Roman Catholic Cistercian   Fax: 03 81 60 44 18
    Contact: Soeur Hotelier

Open To: Individuals, groups, married couples for Retreats and times of reflection and prayer in an atmosphere of silence and peace. Spiritual Direction available. Reservations in writing only. Year round.

Accommodation: Hospitality is provided in the Hotellerie in several rooms. Oratory. Library.

Guests Admitted To: Abbey Church to join the sisters for Mass and the Divine Office sung in French and Gregorian Chant. Monastery Boutique. Audio-visual presentation about monastic life.

Of Interest: Abbaye Notre-Dame de la Grace-Dieu was originally founded by Cistercian monks in 1139. The French Revolution interrupted monastic life, and the monastery suffered much destruction in 1792. Some restoration work was done by the monks in 1845, but they decided to relocate to Tamie (Savoie) in 1909. Cistercian Nuns took up residence in 1927 and continued restoration of the ancient site. The church was renovated in 1997. Part of the building dates back to the *12th c.* Many of the rooms in the abbey and church *(17th – 18th c.)* have been restored to their original beauty. The abbey is located in the picturesque capital of the Franche-Comte close to the Swiss border, and there are countless opportunities for interesting drives and lovely walks.

Access: Rail: Besancon Sta. and Baume-les-Dames (20 km.), then by taxi. Road: Besancon 39 km. Pontarlier 70 km. Belfort 90 km.

Abbaye Notre-Dame de l'Assomption
60138 Chiry-Ourscamp   Tel: 03 44 75 72 14
Roman Catholic   Fax: 03 44 75 72 04
Serviteur de Jesus et de Marie   Contact: Guest Brother

Open To: Individuals, groups for Retreats, and for rest and
renewal. Possibility to share in the work of the brothers.

Accommodation: Hospitality is provided in 20 two-bedded
rooms. Dormitory for young people with a group leader.

Guests Admitted To: Abbey Church to join the community for
liturgical services. Grounds.

Of Interest: In 1941 a small group of the Servants of Jesus and
Mary took possession of the historic Ourscamp Abbey, situated
on the edge of the forest close to Noyon. The abbey was founded
in 1129 by twelve Cistercian monks from the Abbey of
Clairvaux, and it flourished into a large community of
approximately seven hundred monks. However, in 1358 a fire
severely damaged the buildings, and only two were restored.
Centuries later, as a result of the French Revolution, the monks
were dispersed and the property sold off. During WWI, German
troops were entrenched here, and the French artillery further
destroyed the site.

Access: Rail: SNCF at Ourscamp or Noyon (Line Paris Gare du
Nord)/Saint-Quentin/Maubeuge). Road: A1 (Paris-Lille), Exit
Chevrieres or Arsy, then N31 to Compiegne and N32, direction
Noyon to Ribecourt. Take D64 for 3 km., then D48.

The Taize Community
71250 Cluny
E-mail:meetings@taize.fr

Tel: 011 333 85 50 30 02
Fax: 011 333 85 50 30 16
Contact: Meetings

Open To: Young people (ages 17 – 30), young families, married couples for Retreats. Retreatants participate in Bible Introductions, small-group sharing, silent reflection, practical tasks. Manual work optional. A week of silence possible with Spiritual Direction. No sightseeing.

Accommodation: Hospitality is provided in dormitories for singles under age 55. Shared rooms for married couples, adults over 55, and the disabled. Few single rooms. Groups are requested to bring tent or caravan if possible. Villages several kilometers away have limited adult accommodations.

Guests Admitted To: Church of Reconciliation for prayer services three times a day. Grounds.

Of Interest: In 1940 Brother Roger founded the Taize Community. It has grown to over one hundred brothers from Catholic, Anglican, Lutheran, and Reformed traditions from over twenty countries. They have committed themselves to the common life and celibacy, and earn their living and share with others entirely through their own work. Since 1966 the Sisters of St. Andrew, who live nearby, share in hospitality work. People come to Taize, a village in eastern France, for personal reasons, knowing it is a place where one may seek direction in Christ.

Access: Rail: Stations Chalon-sur-Saone, Macon-ville, or Macon-TGV. Take SNCF Bus which connects to Taize. Road: 10 km. north of Cluny on D981. From north, Exit A6 at Chalon-Sud or Tournus. From south, Exit Macon-Sud.

Monastere de Sainte-Claire
53, rue des Auberts
26400 Crest
Roman Catholic, Les Moniales Clarisses

Tel: 0475 25 49 13
Contact: Mother Abbess

Open To: Individuals, groups, families for Retreats, and for those seeking a time apart for prayer and rest in a peaceful environment. Advance reservations required.

Accommodation: Hospitality is provided in the Hotellerie in 25 bedrooms, sink in each room (100 persons). Showers and bathrooms each floor. Conference rooms. Also, small self-catering apartment available. Guests are welcome for a few hours to a max. of 10 days.

Guests Admitted To: Chapel to join the nuns for Mass and the Divine Office. Monastic Shop (products from the gardens – aromatic plants, lavender, jams and jellies). Grounds.

Of Interest: This Poor Clare Monastery dates back to 1843. Throughout its history, there have been periods when it has flourished as well as difficult times. The buildings were remodeled in 1946, and the Hotellerie, dedicated to St. Joseph, was added in 1982. Although originally located in the country, the monastery is now absorbed into the suburbs of the city.

Access: Rail: Line Valence-Veynes. At Valence, by car or train to Crest. Road: Loriol 17 km. Valence 30 km., Exit A7.

Foyer de Charite
La Grand Cour en Tressaint
B. P. 145
22104 Dinan Cedex
E-mail:foyer.tressaint@wanadoo.fr.
Roman Catholic

Tel: 02 96 85 86 00
Fax: 02 96 85 03 56
Contact: Father of the Foyer

Open To: Individuals, groups for Silent Retreats, sharing in the life of the community.

Accommodation: Hospitality is provided in the Retreat House. The Community of Tressaint also has another house for holidays, or a time of rest and convalescence, at the seaside in Brittany near Saint Malo and Mont-Saint-Michel. Contact Foyer de Charite at Tressaint for further info. about Maison Saint-Francois, located at 1, ave. des Acacias, B. P. 100, La Vicomte, 35802 Dinard Cedex, France.

Guests Admitted To: Chapel for Mass, morning and evening prayers, Rosary. Adoration of the Blessed Sacrament.

Of Interest: Foyer de Charite at Tressaint was founded in 1966, one of seventy worldwide. These Catholic lay communities follow the example of the early Christians and place their material, intellectual, and spiritual goods in common. In the same spirit, they are committed to build, with Our Blessed Mother, the family of God on earth, with charity toward one another, and under the spiritual leadership of a priest. Their life of prayer and work bears witness to the teachings of Jesus Christ.

Access: Road: Rennes 50 km.

Sanctuaire Notre-Dame-de-Mont-Roland
B. P. 246   Tel: 03 84 79 88 00
39103 Dole Cedex   Fax: 03 84 79 88 25
Roman Catholic   Contact: Le Recteur

Open To: Individuals, groups for Pilgrimages, Days of Recollection, Meetings, Retreats, and for rest and reflection at certain times of the year.

Accommodation: Hospitality is provided in the Hotellerie in 60 bedrooms, half-board. House chapel, meeting rooms, dining rooms, recreation room, library. The Youth Hostel has 3 dormitories (40 beds) and 7 bedrooms (24 beds). Conference rooms. Send for current rates.

Guests Admitted To: Sanctuary Church of Our Lady of Mont-Roland. Annual Pilgrimage: Aug. 2nd. Portuguese Annual Pilgrimage: Second Sunday of May.

Of Interest: The Sanctuary of Our Lady of Mont-Roland is located in the Jura Mountains. It is one of the oldest pilgrimage centers in the Franche-Comte region as well as a center of Christian formation. Benedictine Monks had a Priory here for nine hundred years. The chapel was destroyed many times due to wars, and was rebuilt in the mid-1800's by Jesuits who had operated a college in Dole since 1582.

Access: Rail: Dole Sta., then 4 km. by taxi. Road: A36, Exit Dole. A39, Exit Dole.

Abbaye Notre-Dame de Sept-Fons   Tel: 33 04 70 48 14 90
03290 Dompierre-Sur-Besbre   Contact: Guestmaster
Roman Catholic Cistercian of the Strict Observance (Trappist)

Open To: Individuals, groups, families for Retreats. Spiritual Direction available. Day visitors welcome. Reception facilities with audio-visual display.

Accommodation: Hospitality is provided in the Guest House in 27 single bedrooms for retreatants and 18 rooms for families, religious and groups. Dining room, chapel.

Guests Admitted To: Abbey Church to join the monks for Mass and the Divine Office. Library. Gift Shop (homegrown products, jams, jellies, and other products).

Of Interest: In 1098 Benedictine Monks from Molesme in Champagne founded the Abbey of Citeaux in the forests south of Dijon. Citeaux founded the Abbey of Clairvaux in 1115, which founded the Abbey of Fontenay in 1118 at Bourgogne. Abbaye Notre-Dame de Sept-Fons was founded by Fontenay in 1132. It was a humble monastery and, in time, fell into ruins. In 1656 the young monk Eustache of Beaufort was named abbot. He began a reform, and the monastery experienced great fervor and growth. The present buildings date back to this restoration, finished in 1789. In 1791, due to the atrocities of the French Revolution, the monks were exiled and suffered a great deal. Sixty four martyrs of Rochefort were beautified by Pope Paul II in 1995. The monks repurchased Sept-Fons in 1845 and have maintained a spiritual presence since. They work in agriculture and have a mill, making a variety of food additives based on germalyne, a wheat/wheat-germ product.

Access: Rail: Sta. Dompierre-Sept-Fons, Line 567, then 4 km. by taxi. Also, Sta. Moulins. Road: D12 or 488. Dompierre 4 km. Moulins 31 km.

Abbaye d'En Calcat
81110 Dourgne
Roman Catholic Benedictine

Tel: 05 63 50 84 70
Fax: 05 63 50 34 90
Contact: Guestmaster

Open To: Individuals, groups, couples for Retreats and other spiritual purposes. Groups bring their own leader and program. Spiritual Direction available. Reservations required.

Accommodation: Hospitality is provided in the Hotellerie for women, young ladies, couples, and religious in 10 single bedrooms, all with bathroom and shower, and in 13 double rooms (2 for the handicapped). Two conference rooms, oratory, refectory. The monastery can accommodate men in 35 single rooms with sinks. Conference room, refectory, oratory. Two dormitories for youth groups are located in The Grange for up to 30 persons. Community bathrooms/showers, gathering room, self-catering kitchen. Max. length of stay one week.

Guests Admitted To: Abbey Church to join the monks for liturgical services. Audio-visual presentation about the abbey and monastic life. Cloistered area off limits to visitors.

Of Interest: Abbaye d'En Calcat was founded in 1890. An atmosphere of silence is encouraged. The Hotellerie is situated near the monastery.

Access: Rail: SNCF – Toulouse-Castres (Ligne de Mazamet), then taxi or bus from Castres Sta. From Carcassonne Sta. take Bus Line d'Albi. Road: D85 – Dourgne 1.5 km. Soual 7 km. Castres and Revel 15 km. D2, N622, D85 from Toulouse, 75 km.

Abbaye Sainte-Scholastique	Tel: 63 50 31 32
81110 Dourgne	Fax: 63 50 12 18
Roman Catholic Benedictine	Contact: Soeur Hoteliere

Open To: Individuals for Retreats. Spiritual Direction available.

Accommodation: Hospitality is provided in the Hotellerie in single bedrooms, some with shower, and in 5 six-bedded dormitories. Bathrooms each floor. Chapel, library, dining room. Max. stay 8 days – longer in June, July, October.

Guests Admitted To: Abbey Church to join the sisters for liturgical services in French and Gregorian Chant. Public welcome. Audio-visual presentation on their life. Monastic Boutique (products from this and other monasteries).

Of Interest: The Abbey of St. Scholastica was founded in 1890 and is situated near the village. The sisters lead a life of prayer and study, work in their print shop, book bindery, make woven goods and liturgical vestments.

Access: Air: Toulouse-Blagnac, then a 60 km. drive – D2, N622, D85. Rail: SNCF: To Castres Sta. (Autorail Toulouse/Castres), then 17 km. by taxi or bus. From Carcassonne Sta., bus d'Albi 50 km. to monastery.

Abbaye Notre-Dame de Bonne Esperance
24410 Echourgnac   Tel: 05 53 80 82 50
Roman Catholic Trappistines   Fax: 05 53 80 08 36
                              Contact: Soeur Hoteliere

Open To: Individuals, groups who desire a time apart in a
monastic setting for spiritual renewal. Advance reservations
suggested.

Accommodation: Hospitality is provided in the Hotellerie in
25 single bedrooms, with showers in the abbey. Two five-bedded
dormitories available in another building. Conference rooms.
Meals available. Max. stay 10 days.

Guests Admitted To: Abbey Church to join the nuns for
liturgical services. Divine Office in French; Gregorian Chant
during Eucharist. Monastic Boutique. Grounds that are open
to guests.

Of Interest: The Abbey of Our Lady of Good Hope was
originally founded in 1868 by Trappist Monks from Port-du-
Salut, Mayenne region. It was abandoned in 1910. Cistercian
Nuns refounded the monastery in 1923, instilling renewed life
into this 'house of prayer'. They support themselves by cheese-
making, sold mainly on the premises at set hours, and in the
region. They also make fruit bars, preserves, and pate de
campagne.

Access: Air: Merignac 100 km., then by train or taxi.
Rail: Montpon 15 km. Mussidan 18 km. St. Aigulin 22 km.
Road: N85 and N708 Montpon-Riberac. Bordeaux 90 km.

Belvedere St.-Dominique   Tel/Fax: 33 04 68 24 72 36
11270 Fanjeaux   Contact: Guest Sister
Roman Catholic Dominican

Open To: Individuals, groups for Retreats, and to make a
Dominican Pilgrimage. Reservations required.

Accommodation: Hospitality is provided in the Retreat House in 22 bedrooms. Bathrooms and showers each floor. Dining room, conference room.

Guests Admitted To: Chapel. St. Dominic's chapel and bedroom. Church of Fanjeaux. Convent of the Preachers *(13th – 14ᵗʰ c.)*. Monastery of Prouille, founded by St. Dominic.

Of Interest: One Dominican Community of Brothers and three of Sisters are located in this small village where St. Dominic, founder of the Order of Preachers, carried out his priestly duties between 1206 and 1215. He preached against heretics of the Middle Ages who had invaded the south of France and northern Italy. Through his teaching, the people were inspired to return to the Church.

Access: Rail: Sta. Bram, then 11 km. by taxi. Sta. Castelnaudary, then 17 km. Road: Autoroute, Exit Bram. Carcassonne 25 km. Toulouse 80 km.

Monastere Sainte-Marie de Prouilhe
11270 Fanjeaux   Tel: 68 24 70 64
Roman Catholic Dominican   Fax: 04 68 24 77 97
                                                   Contact: Prioress

Open To: Pilgrims, the public for Pilgrimages and liturgical services.

Accommodation: Locally.

Guests Admitted To: Chapel to join the sisters for Mass and the Divine Office. St. Dominic's house. Annual Pilgrimage at the Church of Notre-Dame-de-Prouilhe on the first Sunday of October.

Of Interest: Monastere Sainte-Marie de Prouilhe was founded in 1206 by St. Dominic who desired to have a Dominican Order of contemplative nuns to be at the heart of his teaching and preaching ministry. In 1206, on the Feast of St. Mary Magdalen, he prayed on a hilltop in Fanjeaux, asking Our

Blessed Mother for help, as he was unsure about his preaching mission. Suddenly a ball of fire appeared in the sky, hovered, then streaked down to rest above the neglected little Church of Prouilhe. The vision occurred for two more nights, a sure sign from heaven that this area was to be central to his preaching. The Order of Dominican Friars was founded in 1215 at Toulouse.

Access: Rail: SNCF: Bram Sta., Bordeaux-Marseille Line, then by taxi. Road: N119 from Toulouse or Carcassonne.

L'Abbaye Saint-Joseph de Clairval   Tel: 03 80 96b 22 31
21150 Flavigny-sur-Ozerain   Fax: 03 80 96 25 29
Roman Catholic Benedictine   Contact: Guestmaster

Open To: Individuals, groups for Mass and the Divine Office seven times a day in Latin and Gregorian Chant, for those who wish to partake in the monastic life of prayer. Five-Day Ignatian Retreats in French for men only.

Accommodation: Hospitality is provided in the Monastery Guest House. Meals taken with the monks in the refectory. Possible accommodations for ladies in village houses nearby.

Guests Admitted To: Abbey Church. Monastic Gift Shop.

Of Interest: The Abbey of St. Joseph of Clairval was founded in 1972 in Switzerland and transferred to Flavigny in 1976. It is situated on eight hectares of land in this small hilltop town. Part of the monastic day is devoted to sacred doctrine and redaction and mailing of monthly letters devoted to the Catholic faith. The monks perform many maintenance duties on the buildings and grounds, and are engaged in remunerative activities such as fabrication of aluminum windows, composition of texts, icons, and sculpting.

Access: Rail: Sta. Laumes-Alesia 9 km. Sta. Montbard 25 km. Road: Autoroute Paris-Lyon, Exit Bierre-les-Semur, then 22 km. 60 km. northwest of Dijon on D905, then D9.

Abbaye Notre-Dame du Pesquie   Tel: 05 61 02 97 55
Serres-sur-Arget   Fax: 05 61 65 64 71
09000 Foix   Contact: Soeur Hoteliere
Roman Catholic Benedictine

Open To: Priests and nuns for Retreats. Young women discerning a call to religious life. Visitors welcome for liturgical services. Office sung in Latin and Gregorian Chant. Contact Abbess for time schedule.

Of Interest: Abbaye Notre-Dame du Pesquie is situated in the Pyrenees amidst the hills of the Valley of the Barguilliere in Ariege. The sisters have a farm with a fruit orchard, vegetable garden, and apiary. They make cheese, ceramics, liturgical ornaments, and have a book bindery. Honey and other products from their farm are sold at the abbey.

Access: Rail: To Foix Sta., then by taxi. Road: At Foix, take direction of St.-Pierre de Riviere, then D11 in direction of St.-Martin de Caralp. At 2.7 km., on the left a cross indicates the entrance to the short road leading to the abbey. Foix 10 km.

Abbaye Notre-Dame de Fontgombault
36220 Fontgombault   Tel: 54 37 12 03
Roman Catholic Benedictine   Fax: 54 37 12 56
Congregation of Solesmes   Contact: Guestmaster

Open To: Men for Retreats. Public welcome for liturgical services.

Accommodation: Hospitality is provided for retreatants in the Guest House for a few days.

Guests Admitted To: Abbey Church to join the monks for Mass and the Divine Office sung in Latin Gregorian Chant. Chapel of St.-Benoit de Decene. Monastery Shop (cassettes of Gregorian Chant, craft items, farm products, religious articles). Grounds that are open to guests.

Of Interest: The Abbey of Our Lady of Fontgombault was founded in 1948 from the Abbey Saint-Pierre de Solesmes, Sarthe, France. It was elevated to the rank of abbey in 1953. Since the *11th c.,* from a humble hermitage on the other side of the River Creuse there arose a long line of men who strove to embrace community life following the Rule of St. Benedict.

Access: Road: N151 or D975 to LeBlanc, then D950 and follow signs for the abbey. LeBlanc 8 km.

Prieure du Sacre-Coeur
43A, rue du Pont-Rouge
59236 Frelinghien
Roman Catholic Oblates de L'Eucharistie

Tel: 03 20 10 39 39
Fax: 03 20 10 39 69
Contact: Soeur Hoteliere

Open To: Individuals, groups for Retreats in a climate of silence and meditation for spiritual renewal. Advance reservations required.

Accommodation: Hospitality is provided in the Hotellerie in 11 single, 2 double, 1 three-bedded, and 1 family room. Bathrooms each floor. Conference room, dining rooms. Length of stay 1 – 10 days.

Guests Admitted To: Chapel to join the sisters for Mass and the Divine Office. Daily Adoration of the Blessed Sacrament. Grounds.

Of Interest: The Congregation of Oblates of the Eucharist was founded in 1932 at St.-Germain en Laye near Paris. The Priory of the Sacred Heart was founded in 1962 at Frelinghien, a village in northern France near the Belgian border, fifteen kilometers from Lille. This 'house of prayer' is kept by nuns of contemplative life. It is surrounded by a park of one and one-half hectares.

Access: Air: Lille-Lesquin Airport, then 25 km. to Priory. Rail: Sta. Lille-Europe or Sta. Lille-Flandre, then by taxi. Also, may take train from Lille to Armentieres, then bus/taxi 8 km. Road: Autoroute Paris-Bruxelles; Lille-Dunkerque; Lille-Tournai.

Communaute de Caulmont
76400 Froberville
Ecumenical

Tel: 02 35 27 31 72
Fax: 02 35 27 36 67
Contact: Bernard or
Myriam

Open To: Individuals, groups, couples, families for Retreats, Conferences, Sessions, and Vacations.

Accommodation: Hospitality is provided in the Guest House in single, double and family bedrooms (50 beds). Shower and bathroom each floor, and in some rooms. Elevator. Dining room, library, conference room, etc.

Guests Admitted To: Chapel for daily prayer. Extensive grounds.

Of Interest: Caulmont has been in existence since 1970, and the community consists of Christians from different traditions who wish to live according to the spirit of the beatitudes. A number of the residents are available to help guests plan their stay. The house is situated three kilometers from the sea in natural surroundings that are conducive to prayer and a healthful time apart.

Access: Air: Le Havre Airport, then by train or taxi 35 km. Rail: Sta. Fecamp, then 7 km. by bus or taxi. Road: D925 from Dieppe to Fecamp, then D940 Etretat-Fecamp to Froberville. From Le Havre, A13 then A29, Exit in direction of Etretat.

Abbaye Sainte-Marie du Mont-des-Cats
59270 Godewaersvelde
Roman Catholic Cistercian

Tel: 03 28 42 52 50
Fax: 03 28 42 54 80
Contact: Pere Hotelier

Open To: Individuals, groups for Retreats. Spiritual Direction availble. Church open to the public.

Accommodation: Hospitality is provided in the Hotellerie.

Guests Admitted To: Abbey Church to join the monks for liturgical services. Gift Shop.

Of Interest: The Abbey of Our Lady of Mont-des-Cats was founded in 1826 by an artist, Nicolas-Joseph-Ruyssen, and monks from l'Abbaye du Gard, Somme, France. It is situated in French Flanders close to the Belgian border, halfway between Lille and Dunkirk. Originally the monks resided in old buildings on the property. In 1891 they built the actual monastery in *13th c.* Gothic style. However, the site proved to be of strategic importance in WWI, and the monastery was bombed. Only a portion of the wall remained. It was rebuilt on the foundation of the ruins but with simpler furnishings. The church was bombed again during WWII. Over the years the monks have engaged in farming, and ran a brewery until 1907. Today the main source of income comes from their cheese factory. This peaceful spot is set on a large Flanders Plain, and WWI cemeteries of Ieper and Kemmel are nearby.

Access: Rail: SNCF: Sta. Hazebrouck, then 15 km. by bus Hazebrouck/Abeele – runs to Godewaersvelde twice a day. Road: A25, Exit 12 (Meteron). Located halfway on Autoroute Lille-Dunkirk, 20 km. northwest of Armentieres.

Bethanie	Tel: 03 87 52 02 28
Prieure Notre-Dame and Saint-Thiebault	
57680 Gorze	Fax: 03 87 69 91 79
Orthodox	Contact: Secretary

Open To: Individuals, couples for Sessions. No children during organized sessions. Schedule sent upon request. Participation in community tasks required for an hour a day. Only French spoken.

Accommodation: Hospitality is provided in the Hotellerie in two and three-bedded rooms (100 beds). Meals taken in common in the refectory. Meditation rooms, work rooms.

Guests Admitted To: Church to join the community for liturgical services. Grounds.

Of Interest: Bethany Spirituality Center is situated on six hectares of forested land in a natural park of Lorraine. This small Orthodox Community was founded in 1976 by Fr. Alphonse Goettman and his wife Rachel. The main focus of this monastic lifestyle revolves around meditation and the liturgy.

Access: Rail: To Sta. Noveant, Pagny or Onville (between Nancy and Metz). Pick-up at station possible with advance notice. Road: Exit Metz-Nancy at Fey, in direction of Gorze.

Villa Saint-Gerard
169 bis, rue Auguste Potie
59481 Haubourdin
Roman Catholic Redemptorist

Tel: 03 2007 2461
Fax: 03 2007 9088
Contact: Secretary

Open To: Individuals, groups, families for Retreats, Courses, Conferences, and other spiritual activities aimed at deepening one's Christian faith. Day and residential programs.

Accommodation: Hospitality is provided in the villa in 46 single, 20 double bedrooms. Kitchen, dining room, relaxation room, meeting rooms.

Guests Admitted To: Chapels for daily Mass. Grounds.

Of Interest: Villa Saint-Gerard was established in 1932 by the Redemptorist Congregation whose founder was St. Alphonse de Liguori (1696-1787). He was canonized in 1839 and declared a Doctor of the Church in 1871. Two of his famous writings are Moral Theology and Glories of Mary. The community resides on the premises which is situated on one and a half hectares of park-like grounds.

Access: Air: Lille-Lesquin Airport. Rail: Lille Sta., then by bus. Road: RN41 (Bethune-La Bassee). Lille and Dunkirk 9.6 km.

Abbaye Sainte-Marie de Maumont
16190 Juignac   Tel: 011 33 05 45 60 34 38
Roman Catholic Benedictine   Fax: 011 33 05 45 60 29 02
                           Contact: Soeur Hoteliere

Open To: Women, groups, priests, religious for Spiritual
Retreats or a time of rest. Men for overnight stays only, and
with a letter of recommendation by someone well-known to
the sisters. Spiritual Direction possible. A knowledge of the
French language is advisable.

Accommodation: Hospitality is provided in the Guest House
in single and double bedrooms with sink in each room. Shared
bathrooms and showers. Attic dormitory for youth groups.
Dining room, chapel.

Guests Admitted To: Abbey Church to join the sisters for
Mass and the Divine Office sung in French and Gregorian
Chant. Grounds.

Of Interest: Abbaye Sainte-Marie de Maumont was founded
in the 19th c. at Saint-Jean-d'Angely, and the community
transferred to its present location in 1959. It is situated in a
peaceful forested valley. The sisters bake Communion bread,
sew priests' vestments, bind books, and restore ancient texts.

Access: Rail: SNCF: To Angouleme or Bordeaux, then local
train to Montmoreau on the Angouleme-Bordeaux Line.
Montmoreau Sta. 5 km. Taxi can be sent to meet local train
with advance notice. Road: D24 from Maumont. D674 from
Angouleme (30 km.), or Montmoreau.

Abbaye de La Bussiere   Tel: 03 80 49 02 29
21360 La Bussiere-sur-Ouche   Fax: 03 80 49 05 23
Roman Catholic   Contact: Manager
Property of the Bishop of Dijon

Open To: Individuals, groups for Retreats, Workshops,
Seminars, or simply a time apart to enjoy the peace and beauty

Accommodation: Hospitality is provided in the Abbey Guest House in 50 single and double bedrooms. Conference rooms, meeting rooms. Annex Le Moulin can accommodate 60 persons in rooms with 6 to 8 bunk beds each, and 3 rooms for group leaders. Bathrooms, self-service kitchen, dining room, conference rooms.

Guests Admitted To: Abbey Church *(13th c.)*. Crypt. Chapel *(19th c.)*. Theatre (summer concerts). Grounds.

Of Interest: Abbaye de La Bussiere was founded in 1130 by Cistercian Monks from Citeaux. They were dispersed in 1791 by the forces of the French Revolution and the property was sold. During the *19th c.,* two L-shaped structures were restored. Located in the Valley of the Ouche in the heart of Burgundy, there are over twelve acres for quiet walks among natural surroundings and ancient structures. The abbey is maintained and operated by laymen in cooperation with religious leaders, and is open to all with a broader vision concerning its activities.

Access: Road: A6 from Paris, Dijon Jct. (A38), then D33 at Pont de Pany Exit. A6 or A36 from Lyon or Mulhouse. Bypass Beaune on Ring Rd., then D970 for Bligny sur Ouche. Dijon 32 km. Lyon 190 km.

Sanctuaire Notre-Dame de Montligeon
61400 La Chapelle Montligeon   Tel: 02 33 85 17 00
Roman Catholic, Benedictine Sisters   Fax: 02 33 83 60 49
of the Sacred Heart of Montmartre   Contact:Director General

Open To: Pilgrims, visitors for Pilgrimages, Retreats, and Vacations, for those seeking a warm and peaceful setting for a Spiritual holiday. Guided Tours available. Year round.

Accommodation: Hospitality is provided in l'Ermitage of the Basilica in 29 single, 30 double and 11 family rooms (120 beds). Sanitary facilities each floor. Conference rooms, meeting rooms, TV room. Restaurant seats 800. Length of stay 1 or more nights.

Guests Admitted To: Basilica for liturgical services. Diaporama. Library. Grounds.

Of Interest: The Sanctuary of Our Lady of Montligeon has been an important pilgrimage center for over one hundred years, with a special mission of promoting prayer for the souls in Purgatory. The basilica is a light for many nations as it reaches out to teach believers to be faithful in praying for their deceased loved ones as well as for those who have none to pray for them. In so doing, one is made aware of the Communion of Saints in a real way. The center is located in the heart of the Perche country between Beauce and Normandy. It is surrounded by forests, with opportunities for long, quiet walks.

Access: Rail: Line Paris Montparnasse-Le Mans to Conde-sur-Huisne or Nogent-le-Rotrou, then by bus or taxi. Road: N12 past Dreux and Verneuil, then D5 past Feings. Near Chartres Exit A11 in direction of Nogent-le-Rotrou, Conde-sur-Huisne, and la Chappelle Montligeon.

Carmel de la Sainte Trinite
29, rue de l'Evescot
17000 La Rochelle
Roman Catholic Carmelite

Tel: 05 46 41 47 02
Contact: Abbess

Open To: Young women interested in entering religious life as a Carmelite, and religious actively engaged in ministry for Retreats. Public welcome for liturgical services.

Accommodation: Hospitality is provided in 3 guest rooms in the monastery.

Guests Admitted To: Chapel to join the nuns for Mass and the Divine Office.

Of Interest: This small Carmelite Monastery, 'Le Jardin', was founded in 1858. The chapel is a popular stop for tourists seeking time apart to pray.

Access: Rail: Sta. La Rochelle, then by taxi.

Sanctuaire Notre-Dame de La Salette
38970 La Salette   Tel: 04 76 30 00 11
                                        Fax: 04 76 30 03 65
                                        Contact: Reception Office

Open To: Pilgrims wishing to experience the silence of this isolated Marian Shrine in the French Alps. High Season: Easter – August. Youth groups welcome during school vacations and in July and August. Day Care Center for children. Special youth programs. Small group and individual discussions with priests.

Accommodation: Hospitality is provided in The Inn on site for 650 persons in single rooms with sinks, some double with private baths. Bathrooms and showers each floor. Also, a dormitory and hostel are available. Dining room, cafeteria. Picnics authorized.

Guests Admitted To: Site of the apparition, the Fountain of Our Lady. Shrine Basilica for liturgical services. Candlelight processions. Audio-visual presentations. Museum. Guided Tours. Book and Gift Shop.

Of Interest: La Salette is the site of the Catholic Church-approved apparition of Mary to the two children, Melanie Calvat and Maximin Giraud on September 19, 1846. Missionaries of Our Lady of La Salette, fathers, brothers and sisters maintain the shrine with dedicated lay persons. Side trips of interest: the Pra family home in Les Ablandins where Melanie first reported the vision; birthplace of the visionaries in Corps, and the parish church; climb Mt. Gargas and visit the tunnels. In close proximity: Chapel of Our Lady Reconciler in Grenoble; Vercors Regional Park with its Caverns of Choranche; Grande

Chartreuse Cellars at Voiron, distillery and tasting tour of world famous Chartreuse liquors (Carthusian Monks).

Access: Road: Route Napoleon (RN85). By Autocar (Lines VFD and SCAL). By taxi, Corps/the shrine 15 km. Gap/Corps 40 km. Grenoble/Corps 60 km. July – August only, bus leaves daily from Grenoble to shrine. Road usually open in winter. Call for road conditions prior to ascending mountain. The sanctuary is located eighteen hundred meters above sea level.

Abbaye Notre-Dame de l'Annonciation Tel: 04 90 65 29 29
La Font de Pertus   Contact: Sister in Charge
84330 Le Barroux   of Guest House
Roman Catholic Benedictine

Open To: Women for Private Retreats. Young girls and women wishing to study their vocation. A monk from the neighboring Abbaye Sainte-Madeleine is available for Spiritual Direction.

Accommodation: Hospitality is provided in the Abbey Guest House for retreatants.

Guests Admitted To: Church for all the offices. Tridentine Mass celebrated weekdays 09:00, Sundays and holy days 10:00. Vespers daily at 17:30. Monastic Boutique (homemade products, books, small religious articles).

Of Interest: In 1983, this new abbey began construction in the Southern French style. The sisters devote themselves to a life of prayer, study and work. They cultivate several acres of vineyards and apricot orchards, make jams and candies, and record cassettes of Gregorian Chant. They have edited an illustrated book on the life of St. Benedict, patron of Europe.

Access: Road: From Orange, take Exit Orange-Carpentras-Malaucene. From Avignon, Exit Avignon- N.-Carpentras-Malaucene. The abbey is 2 km. from the Abbey of St. Madeleine and 5 km. from Le Barroux.

Abbaye Sainte-Madeleine
84330 Le Barroux
Roman Catholic Benedictine

Tel: 04 90 62 56 31
Contact: Guestmaster

Open To: Men for Retreats. Spiritual Direction available.
Mixed groups for non-residential Retreats. Public is welcome
for liturgical services.

Accommodation: Hospitality is provided for men in the
abbey's guest wing. Women stay at Maison Francois-Joseph,
600 m. from the abbey.

Guests Admitted To: Abbey Church to join the monks for
Mass and the Divine Office. Book Shop. Abbey Bakery.
Library. Grounds.

Of Interest: Abbaye Sainte-Madeleine was founded in 1970 and
raised to the rank of abbey in 1989. A primary work of the
community is religious instruction and sacramental
preparation.

Access: Rail: Sta. Avignon 48 km. Road: From Orange or
Avignon, Exit Orange – Carpentras – Malaucene.
Le Barroux 3 km.

Monastere de Saint-Nicolas
La Dalmerie
34260 Le Bousquet d'Orb
Greek Orthodox

Tel: 04 67 23 41 10
Contact: Frere Hotelier

Open To: Individuals, groups, pilgrims for Retreats. Spiritual
Direction available. Advance reservations required. Day
visitors welcome and are requested to call ahead.

Accommodation: Hospitality is provided in the Hotellerie for
retreatants.

Guests Admitted To: Byzantine-style Church to join the
monks for Divine Liturgy in French. Special Feast Days: St.
Nicolas - May 20 and December 6.

Of Interest: The Monastery of St. Nicholas was founded in 1962. Its mission is to offer to the Orthodox Christian the French expression of the Orthodox tradition. The monks engage in many activities which enable them to be self sufficient, such as farming, goat herding (*cheese*), icon painting, collages, and wood sculptures. They sell rosaries of wool, votive candles, cards, and edit Orthodox prayer books, books on spirituality, and a brochure about the monastery.

Access: Rail: Sta. Le Bousquet d'Orb, then 16 km. by taxi. Train may stop at Les Cabrils, an isolated stop, 6 km. from monastery. Road: 76 km. from Montpellier, 22 km. from Lodeve on N109, D35, D142, D138. 65 km. north of Beziers on D609N, D35, D8, D138.

Communaute de l'Abbaye du Mont-Saint-Michel
Boite Postale, 3   Tel: 33 60 14 47
50170 Le Mont-Saint-Michel   Fax: 33 60 31 02
E-mail:abbayemichel@wanadoo.fr   Contact: Pere Hotelier
Internet:www.cef.fr/couances
Roman Catholic

Open To: Individuals, small groups for Silent Retreats. Groups need a letter of recommendation from their parish priest specifying reason parishioner wishes to make this retreat. Day visitors/pilgrims contact: Tourist Office – Tel: 33 60 14 30 for details and current fees. One must be in good physical condition as the sanctuary is situated on the summit of the rock with 300 stairs.

Accommodation: Hospitality is provided in the Hotellerie for retreatants. Weekends and weeks directly preceding and following Christmas and Easter – 12 beds available. Mid-week, 3 two-bedded rooms available. Shared bathrooms. Min. stay 2 day; max. stay 7 days. Hotellerie open Tuesday – Sunday.

Guests Admitted To: Basilica to join the community for liturgical services. Retreatants expected to participate in daily Mass and the Divine Office. Liturgy celebrated in French.

Of Interest: The Community of Mont-Saint-Michel consists of brothers and sisters who follow the Rule of St. Benedict. They do not organize visits to the abbey.

Access: Rail: From Paris to Pontorson Sta., then bus or taxi. Mont-St.-Michel 9 km. Line Paris/Brest: Depart Montparnasse Sta., arrive Rennes Sta., then bus (Courriers Bretons) to Mont-St.-Michel 70 km. Line Paris/Cherbourg: Depart St. Lazare Sta., arrive Pontorson Sta. via Caen Sta., then bus or taxi 9 km. Line Paris/Granville: Depart Montparnasse Sta., arrive Pontorson Sta. via Folligny Sta., then bus or taxi 9 km.

Abbaye Notre-Dame des Dombes
01330 Le Plantay
Roman Catholic Cistercian

Tel: 74 98 14 40
Contact: Guestmaster

Open To: Individuals, groups for Silent Retreats. Public welcome for church services.

Accommodation: Hospitality is provided in the Hotellerie for retreatants. Youth groups accommodated in a separate location.

Guests Admitted To: Abbey Church to join the monks for Mass and the Divine Office. Gift Shop (*abbey products – jams, fruit candies, petit fours, and the renowned 'Musculine G'.)* Grounds that are open to retreatants.

Of Interest: The Trappist Abbey of Our Lady of Dombes was founded in 1863 from l'Abbaye d'Aiguebelle. It is situated between the Ain, Rhone and Saone Rivers in a hilly area with thousands of stagnant ponds. Besides their life of prayer and study, the monks have from the beginning worked to dry up the ponds, which were the breeding ground for insects that spread swamp fever. Their efforts gave heart to the afflicted population to do the same, turning unproductive, unhealthy land into adequate soil for cattle and grains. The monks received the Legion of Honor and the War Cross for their contribution resisting the Nazi occupation.

Access: Road: From Bourg, N83, then D22. From Lyon, N83 to Marlieux, then exit in direction of Chalamont. Take D22 to abbey.

Le Domaine de Chadenac
43000 Ceyssac
Le Puy-en-Velay
Union Catholique de Plein Air et des Centres de Vacances

Tel: 04 71 09 27 62
Fax: 04 71 02 87 45
Contact: Director

Open To: Individuals, pilgrims, families, groups for Retreats, Conferences, Meetings, Reunions, Vacations. Family Times: end of June – end of August. Advance reservations needed.

Accommodation: Hospitality is provided in the Guest House for over 100 persons in single, double, and family bedrooms, some en-suite. Conference rooms, meeting rooms, oratory, workshops. Indoor and outdoor dining – extra cost. Day Care: ages 2 – 5 and 6 – 12, M – F, with activities.

Guests Admitted To: Chapel. Grounds. Activity Classes. Sports Tournaments. Guided Walks.

Of Interest: Le Domaine de Chadenac Vacation and Conference Center is situated within a large park in the beautiful Haute-Loire Department, south central France, an area noted for its wide array of sports and leisure activities and excursions. The center offers many activities including archery, pony rides, horseback riding, climbing, canoeing, sailing, and golf.

Access: Air: Le Puy-Loudes Airport, then 5 min. by taxi. Rail: Sta. Le Puy-en-Velay 10 min. away.

Abbaye Notre-Dame de la Grainetiere Tel: 02 51 67 21 19
85500 Les Herbiers   Fax: 02 51 67 21 19
Roman Catholic Benedictine   Contact: Guest Brother
Congregation Notre-Dame d'Esperance

Open To: Individuals, groups, youth, families for visits, picnics, and tours of this ancient abbey. Also, for those desiring a time apart in silence, peace and reflection. Spiritual Dialogue with a member of the community is possible.

Accommodation: Hospitality is provided in the small Hotellerie for up to 4 persons.

Guests Admitted To: Chapel (former Chapter Hall) to join the monks for liturgical services. Grounds.

Of Interest: The Abbey of Our Lady of Grainetiere was originally founded in 1130 by Benedictine Monks from Abbaye Notre-Dame de Fontdouce, Saintonge, France. Up to the *16th c.,* it was attacked many times during various wars. Following the French Revolution, the buildings were abandoned and sold as national goods. The church was used as a stone quary, and the buildings part of a farm. In 1963 the Societe Civile Immobiliere de la Grainetiere bought the remaining buildings and began restoration work. In 1978 monastic life returned to the abbey when the Benedictine Community, founded in 1966 at Croixrault, leased this historic complex. The priests and brothers belong to a congregation founded for men with physical handicaps and/or chronic illnesses. They are happy here in this peaceful, beautiful setting of solitude, situated near a large forest. Their life of prayer, study and work includes fabrication of icons, jewelry-making, and hospitality. There are many opportunities for excursions, including a visit to the Basilica of St.- Laurent-sur-Sevre, which houses the tomb of St. Louis-Marie de Montfort and bienheureuse Louise Marie Trichet.

Access: Road: N148B from Nantes, 70 km., Exit Mortagne S/Sevre. N160 from Les Essarts. Bordeaux 300 km. Paris 400 km.

St. Therese's Basilica   Contact: Pilgrimage Director
Avenue Sainte-Therese
14100 Lisieux
Roman Catholic Carmelite

Open To: Pilgrims wishing to visit this beautiful Sanctuary
Church and other places of importance in the life of St. Theresa.

Guests Admitted To: Basilica (1929). Crypt. Exhibits. Film
'Vrai Visage de Therese de Lisieux' – also in English. Carmel
Chapel for morning Mass. Hall of Relics at Carmel. 'Les
Buissonnets,' – Theresa's childhood home – commentary in
English is recorded.

Of Interest: Therese Martin was born to Louis Martin and
Zelie Guerin Martin on January 2, 1873. At age 15 she entered
the Carmelite Convent at Lisieux and took the name of Sr.
Therese of the Child Jesus and the Holy Face. She described
her life as 'a little way of spiritual childhood,', and believed that
what matters in life is 'not great deeds, but great love.' She died
September 30, 1897, and was canonized May 17, 1925 by Pope
Pius XI. St. Theresa's Basilica is situated between Carmel and
the town cemetery where Theresa was buried until her
exhumation in 1923. She is the second Patroness of France and
the Patroness of Missions. Her autobiography 'THE STORY OF
A SOUL' is suggested reading prior to visiting her shrine. St.
Theresa was proclaimed a Doctor of the Church in 1997. Places
of Interest: house in Alencon where she was born and where her
mother died, two hours from Lisieux (one hundred kilometers);
Church of Notre-Dame where she was baptized and her parents
married; the Lace School – Mrs. Martin was a lace maker; Mr.
Martin's jewelry shop; Church of St.-Pierre de Montsort, the
family's parish for thirteen years.

Access: Road: From Paris, rue de Paris. Take left onto Blvd.
Jean d'Arc. At intersection of Ave. Ste.-Therese and Blvd. Ste.-
Anne, take left. Car parks near basilica. Evreux 72 km. Rouen
82 km. Paris 174 km.

Sanctuaire Notre-Dame de Lourdes   Tel: 05 62 42 78 01
Bureau de Presse   Fax: 05 62 42 78 77
1, Ave. Monseigneur Theas   Contact: Director
65108 Lourdes Cedex
Roman Catholic

Open To: Pilgrims. Pilgrimage Season: April – October.
Winter Season: November – March. Contact for schedule of
events. Forum Information provides all info. for visitors and
audio-visual presentation. Pastoral Information (CAP) registers
and arranges programs for pilgrimages.

Accommodation: Tourism/hotel info. from Tourist Bureau,
Peyramale Sq. (center of town). Several hundred pilgrims with
special needs can be accommodated at Cite Saint-Pierre,
accessible by bus. Campgrounds in the area.

Guests Admitted To: Upper Basilica (1871), built on the Rock
of Massabielle. Sanctuary over the site of the apparitions.
Grounds of the Lourdes World Pilgrimage Center.

Of Interest: Marie Bernarde Soubirous was the eldest child of a
poor miller and his wife. On February 11, 1858, this
uneducated fourteen year old was gathering firewood with
friends. She heard a sound like the wind and saw a light and
the form of a young woman dressed in white, with a blue
cincture, and a yellow rose on each foot. She held a rosary on
her arm and smiled down on the girl, inviting her to pray. Our
Blessed Mother appeared to Bernadette several times, and on
March 25 identified herself as the Immaculate Conception, and
directed the girl to build a chapel here. Bernadette became a
Sister of Notre Dame of Nevers in 1866. Sr. Marie Bernarde
worked with the sick until she became ill. She remained at the
Convent of Nevers near Paris until her death at age 35. Pope
Pius XI canonized her in 1933. Lourdes is located in southwest
France at the foot of the Pyrenee Mountains.

Access: Air: Airport 10 km. from pilgrimage center. Rail: SNCF
Lourdes Sta. Road: Bartres 3 km. Argeles 13 km. Betharram
15 km. Tarbes 19 km.

Ermitage de Saint-Walfroy Tel: 24 22 67 31
08370 Margut Contact: Director
Roman Catholic Brothers of the Auxiliary of Clerge

Open To: Pilgrims, individuals, families who wish to visit this
international pilgrimage center. Advance reservations required.
Schedule of services sent upon request.

Accommodation: Hospitality is provided in the Hotellerie for
64 persons in 14 single, 3 double, 7 two-bedded, and 10 three-
bedded rooms. Two dining rooms *(notify in advance of special
meal requirements)*. Gathering room, conference room.

Guests Admitted To: Church for liturgical services. Chapel of
Notre-Dame. Tomb of St. Walfroy. Resource Center. Gift Shop.

Of Interest: St. Walfroy (565-594) was from the region of
Europe de l'Est. He was a disciple of St. Martin of Tours and
lived an ascetic life. His holiness attracted much attention and
was responsible for many converts to Christianity. In obedience
to his archbishop, he left the hermitage to evangelize the region,
and built a church in the hills that was a center of deep
spirituality for many centuries. This hallowed ground was
consecrated by men who lived the hermitic life of prayer,
fasting, and abstinence, following the example of St. Walfroy.
The hermitage overlooks the countryside of Yvois.

Access: Rail: Carignan Sta. 13 km., then by taxi or bus.
Road: RN43 to Margut. CD44 from La Ferte.

Basilique Notre-Dame de Marienthal Tel: 33 3 88 93 90 91
1, place de la Basilique Fax: 33 3 88 93 97 01
67500 Marienthal Contact: Sister in Charge
Roman Catholic Diocesan Priests and the Benedictine Adorers
of the Sacred Heart of Jesus of Montmartre

Open To: Individuals, groups for Retreats, Pilgrimage, a time
for prayer or meditation, self-organized by the group or by the
Center of Christian Formation. The Benedictine Sisters are a
contemplative and apostolic community founded in 1898.

Accommodation: Hospitality is provided in 23 bedrooms with wash basins. Shared showers/bathrooms. Five double rooms with showers/bathrooms. Meeting rooms, dining room. Length of stay one day to a month.

Guests Admitted To: Basilica to participate in the prayer life of the sanctuary, and to join the sisters for Mass and the Divine Office. Adoration of the Blessed Sacrament. Religious Gift Shop.

Of Interest: Marienthal was founded in 1250 by the noble Knight Albert of Haguenau. It has been a place of pilgrimage since the *13th c.*, and is the most famous Marian Shrine in Alsace. The basilica is surrounded by a large park near the forest called Holy Forest. Places of interest: picturesque villages of the North Alsace; the Vosges Mountains; Strasbourg, European capital; the Black Forest.

Access: Air: Strasbourg Entzheim Airport (Paris-Strasbourg). Rail: Strasbourg-Haguenau. Road: Paris-Strasbourg, Exit Haguenau.

Basilique Notre-Dame de la Garde
13281 Marseille Cedex 6
E-mail:ndgarde@marseilles.com
Roman Catholic

Tel: 4 91 13 40 80
Fax: 4 91 37 28 99
Contact: Recteur

Open To: Pilgrims/visitors wishing to attend church services and special devotions. Guided Tours available. Contact for further information.

Accommodation: Restaurant/cafeteria.

Guests Admitted To: Roman-Byzantine style Basilica (1864). Audio-visual presentation. Crypt. Gallery. Religious Gift Shop. Library run by the Franciscan Missionary Sisters of Mary.

Of Interest: In 1214 a chapel was built on the Hill of Notre-Dame de la Garde in honor of Our Blessed Mother. It was rebuilt in 1477, and was surrounded by fortifications in 1525. The foundation stone was laid for the basilica in 1853. The silver statue of Mary was made in 1833 and sets on the high altar. The monumental Statue of the Tower (1870), the work of Duquesne, sets on its pedestal, the 'Good Mother with Child Jesus' protecting the city, missionaries, sailors and travelers. The 'Great Bell' has rung since 1845, announcing special times for prayer and liturgical services. There is a beautiful panoramic view of the Harbor of Marseilles and the islands beyond from this bastion of spirituality.

Access: Good public transport.

Chartreuse Notre-Dame de Montrieux
83136 Meounes   Tel: 94 48 98 10
Roman Catholic Order of Carthusian   Contact: Le Pere Recteur

Open To: Young men who are discerning a vocation to monastic life for Retreats, to pray, live and work with the monks. Request made in writing giving specific reasons for choosing this lifestyle. Pilgrims/visitors are welcome for church services. Family members may stay twice a year.

Accommodation: Hospitality is provided for families of the monks in the Hotellerie. Young men reside in cells – usual length of stay a few days to a few weeks.

Guest Admitted To: Chapel to join the monks for Mass and the Liturgy of the Hours. Grounds that are open to guests.

Of Interest: Chartreuse de Montrieux was founded in 1137, fifty years after the founding of the Carthusian Order. The community has a novitiate for young men who wish to embrace this life of prayer, taking vows of celibacy and poverty. The monks live in solitude in their hermitages, ever mindful through prayer and meditation, of the needs of suffering humanity. They support themselves through agricultural work, their orchard, and apiary. They also do woodworking, metal work, bookbinding, and bake bread.

Access: Rail: SNCF: Sta. Toulon-Brignoles, stop Martinet-de-Montrieux, then 2 km. to the monastery. Road: N97, N554, D202. Toulon 21 km.

Monastere Notre-Dame
2, rue Madame Curie
Charleville-Mezieres
08000 Montcy Saint-Pierre
Roman Catholic Benedictine

Tel: 03 24 59 01 11
Contact: Frere Hotelier

Open To: Individuals for Spiritual Retreats.

Accommodation: Hospitality is provided in the Hotellerie in 4 bedrooms, 2 bathrooms. Conference rooms. Max. stay 1 – 5 d.

Guests Admitted To: Chapel to join the monks for Mass and the Divine Office. Grounds.

Of Interest: Monastere Notre-Dame is situated on one hectare of parklike grounds, with opportunities for pleasant walks along the Meuse and Semois Rivers.

Access: Rail: SNCF: Charleville Sta., then 2 km. by bus or taxi.

Notre-Dame de Myans
Centre Spirituelle
73800 Montmelian
Roman Catholic Diocesan Priests

Tel: 79 28 11 65
Contact: Rector

Open To: Individuals, groups for Pilgrimage, Retreats, Days of Recollection, Conferences, Meetings.

Accommodation: Hospitality is provided in La Maison de Rencontres Spirituelles in single and double rooms (50 beds). Oratory, 2 conference rooms, meeting rooms, dining room.

Guests Admitted To: Original Chapel. Sanctuary Church (1498). Crypt Chapel. Grounds.

Of Interest: The Marian Sanctuary of Notre-Dame de Myans dates back to 1100 when a chapel was built here. It is situated on a hilltop at the foot of Mount Granier in the Savoie region, overlooking the Valley of Chambery at Mont Melian, an area rich in vineyards. In 1248 Mount Granier was devastated by an earthquake, and sixteen villages with thousands of people were buried. The chapel was miraculously spared. A Franciscan Convent was founded here in the *15th c.,* but during the French Revolution the monks were dispersed and the sanctuary destroyed. Today diocesan priests maintain the pilgrimage center, assisted by lay persons and religious. Retired priests who have ministered here reside in one of the houses.

Access: Air: Vogland (Aix-Chambery), then by taxi. Rail: Sta. Chambery 10 km. Sta. Montmelian 2 km. Road: A43. N6.

Centre Spirituel du Hautmont
31, rue Mirabeau, B. P. 19
59420 Mouvaux
Roman Catholic Jesuit

Tel: 03 20 26 09 61
Fax: 03 20 11 26 59
Contact: Director

Open To: Individuals, groups, couples for Retreats, Spiritual Formation Courses, Reunions, Seminars conducted by a team of priests and laymen. Day and residential use. Program sent on request.

Accommodation: Hospitality is provided in the center in 46 bedrooms with wash basins, single and double (87 beds). Tubs/bathrooms each floor. Two conference rooms, 14 meeting rooms, workroom, dining room.

Guests Admitted To: Chapel. Grounds.

Of Interest: Centre Spirituel du Hautmont is located in the heart of the metropolis of Lille in northern France. It is situated on seven hectares of park like grounds. Places of interest within close proximity are the cities of Gand, Bruges, and Brussells in Belgium.

Access: Air: Lesquin Airport 25 km. Rail: Sta. Lille 10 km. Sta. Roubaix 5 km., then by bus or taxi. Road: A22.

Carmel
35, rue des Montapins
58000 Nevers
Roman Catholic Carmelite

Tel: 86 57 09 75
Contact: Prioress

Open To: Apostolic sisters wishing a time apart for rest and spiritual renewal. Spiritual Direction available.

Accommodation: Hospitality is provided in 2 rooms in the monastery. Max. stay one weekend to a few days.

Guests Admitted To: Chapel to join the nuns for Mass and the Divine Office in French.

Of Interest: Carmel of Nevers was founded in 1619, and transferred to its present location in 1966. Besides their life of prayer, the nuns bake altar bread, and they create infants' sponge texture clothes and stuffed animals. The Shrine of St. Bernadette Soubirous at St. Gildard's Convent, a twenty minute walk from Carmel, is situated in the center of Nevers.

Access: Rail: SNCF: Nevers Sta., then Bus Line 4A.
Road: Bourges 60.8 km.

Saint- Gildard   Tel: 03 86 71 99 50
34, rue Saint-Gildard   Fax: 03 86 71 99 51
58000 Nevers   Contact: Director
Roman Catholic Sisters of Charity of Nevers

Open To: Individuals, groups for Retreats, Pilgrimage.
Spiritual Direction available. Special Masses for groups with
prior notice.

Accommodation: Hospitality is provided in the House of
Spirituality and Pilgrimage Center for 200 persons in single,
double, two-bedded, and three-bedded rooms. Showers and
bathrooms each floor. Refectories, dining rooms, conference
rooms, meeting rooms, oratories.

Guests Admitted To: Main Chapel and the Shrine of St.
Bernadette. Other chapels. Museum. A spiritual march,
'Walking in the Steps of Bernadette,' accompanied by a team of
sisters, through the significant places in her life at Saint-
Gildard, to discover the way of the Gospel that she advocates.
Gift Shop. Special Feast Days: Feb. 11 – first vision of Our
Lady of Lourdes; Feb. 18 – St. Bernadette.

Of Interest: Saint-Gildard was a holy priest who resided in the
vicinity of Nevers in the 7th c. In 1853 the Mother House of the
Sisters of Charity of Nevers was built on the site of an ancient
abbey that had been founded near the town walls and named
after Saint-Gildard. Bernadette Soubirous sought admission to
the Convent of St.-Gildard in 1866 and remained here, living a
life of simplicity and holiness, until her death in 1879. In 1925
her body was found to be intact, and it was transported to the
main chapel. She was canonized December 8, 1933.

Access: Rail: Nevers Sta., 500 m. from St.-Gildard. Road: A6
from Paris, then N151 at Auxerre. N79 from Macon, then N9.
D973 from Beaune, then N9.

Monastere des Clarisses de Nimes-Alger   Contact: Abbess
34, rue de Brunswick
30000 Nimes
Roman Catholic, Franciscan Order of St. Clare

Open To: Individuals, groups, married couples for Retreats, or simply a time apart in a monastic setting. Spiritual Direction available.

Accommodation: Hospitality is provided in the Hostel in 10 rooms. Shared showers/bathrooms. Meals provided for small groups. Kitchen available to guests for self-catering.

Guests Admitted To: Chapel to join the nuns for liturgical services. Grounds.

Of Interest: The Poor Clare Monastery of Nimes-Algeria was founded in 1240. It is situated east of this ancient city in southern France. Nearly all the nuns fled hostilities in Algeria in 1995 to settle in this large monastery with the few nuns that had been praying for others to join them.

Access: Rail: SNCF: Nimes Sta., then by car or bus.
Road: Marseilles 102.4 km.

Monastere Marthe et Marie de Bethanie
Domaine de Burtin   Tel: 00 33 (0) 2 54 88 77 33
41600 Nouan-le-Fuzelier   Fax: 00 33 (0) 2 54 88 97 73
Roman Catholic   Contact: Guest Sister
Communaute des Beautitudes

Open To: Individuals, groups, couples, priests, religious, families, youth for Retreats in an atmosphere of silence and meditation. Spiritual Direction available. Priest available for Confession. With prior arrangement, an individual may spend an extended length of time sharing in the life of the community.

Accommodation: Hospitality is provided in monastery guest rooms. Meals taken in common with the community.

Guests Admitted To: Monastery Church to join the community for liturgical services. Perpetual Adoration of the Blessed Sacrament. Grounds. Conference twice a day for retreats.

Of Interest: The Monastery of Martha and Mary of Bethany was founded in 1983. The brothers and sisters share a life of liturgy and service, their main mission being evangelization through retreat work. The monastery is surrounded by park like grounds and forests in the heart of Sologne, close to the village of Nouan-le-Fuzelier.

Access: Rail: Sta. Nouan-le-Fuzelier. Pickup at station possible with advance notice. Road: RN20 or A71, Exit Lamotte-Beuvron. Approx. 38 km. from Vierzon. Orleans 45 km. Paris 170 km.

Hotellerie du Mont Sainte-Odile
67530 Ottrott
Roman Catholic Diocesan Priests
Soeurs de La Croix

Tel: 33 03 88 95 80 53
Fax: 33 03 88 95 82 96
Contact: Soeur Hoteliere

Open To: Individuals, groups, families for Pilgrimages, and for those wishing a time for rest and renewal in a spiritual setting. Advance booking suggested.

Accommodation: Hospitality is provided in the Hotellerie in 140 bedrooms. Meeting rooms, reading room, dining rooms. Restaurant with regional specialties.

Guests Admitted To: Monastery Church *(17th c.)*. Pilgrims Hall. Chapel of the Cross *(11th c.)*. St. Odile's Chapel and Tomb *(8th c.)*. Chapel of the Tears. Chapel of the Angels *(11th c.)*. Grounds, including St. Odile's Source, Grotto of Lourdes, Way of the Cross, and remnants of 9.6 km. pagan wall *(1000 B.C.)*.

Of Interest: St. Odile *(7th c.)* founded a monastery in Altitona, which was destroyed and rebuilt many times over the years until the nuns were finally forced to leave in 1546 following a devastating fire. The tomb of Sainte-Odile became a revered place of pilgrimage due to the efforts of Premontres priests; however, during the French Revolution, they were forced to flee. Mont Sainte-Odile was restored in 1853 by the Bishop of Strasbourg. The pilgrimage center is situated in the Bloss Mountains, and there are magnificent views of the Alsace Plain, Strasbourg, the Black Forest, the Rhine and the Vosges.

Access: Air: Strasbourg-Entzheim Airport 30 km. Rail: Sta. Obernai 12.8 km., or Sta. Barr 12 km., Line Strasbourg-Molsheim-Selestat, then by taxi. Road: D422 from Molsheim, direction of Obernai to N422, Exit Barr. From Selestat, A35, N422, Exit Barr. A352 from Strasbourg 40 km. Colmar 49.6 km. Buses run from Easter to October.

Abbaye Sainte-Marie
3, rue de la Source
75016 Paris
Roman Catholic Benedictine

Tel: 45 25 30 07
Contact: Guestmaster

Open To: Men seeking a time apart in silence and solitude while on Retreat for a few days. Day groups, men and women, may use the monastery's facilities for Seminars, Conferences.

Accommodation: Hospitality is provided in the Hotellerie for men on retreat.

Guests Admitted To: Abbey Church to join the monks for Mass and the Divine Office, sung in Gregorian Chant. Library, open W – Sat. *(17:00 – 18:00)* and *(18:30 – 19:00),* and Sundays *(11:15 – 12:15).* Grounds that are open to guests.

Of Interest: Abbaye Sainte-Marie was founded in 1893. The library has over one million books and periodicals, available for spiritual reading by retreatants at set times.

Access: Rail: Metro Line Jasmin. Autobus 22, 52, 62, Line C*Javel, *Pdt-Kennedy, *Boulainvilliers.

Chapel of Our Lady of the Miraculous Medal
140, rue du Bac   Tel: 33 1 49 54 78 78
75340 Paris Cedex 7
Roman Catholic, Daughters of Charity of St. Vincent de Paul

Open To: Pilgrims from around the world, for Mass and private devotions. On Tuesdays, prior to 12:30 Mass, prayers are offered for the granting of petitions collected the previous day by one of the sisters.

Guests Admitted To: Chapel of Our Lady of the Miraculous Medal. Altar and Shrine of St. Louise de Marillac, co-founder with St. Vincent of the Daughters of Charity. To the right of the main altar – incorrupt body of St. Catherine Laboure, exhumed in 1933, fifty seven years after her death. She was canonized in 1947.

Of Interest: In 1830 St. Catherine Laboure received the grace of apparitions of the Blessed Virgin Mary in the community's chapel, and was asked by Our Lady to have a medal struck showing her image in honor of the Immaculate Conception. This medal became the famous 'Miraculous Medal.' Catherine's confessor, Fr. Aladel, the only one to whom she revealed the apparitions until a few months before her death, secured permission from the Archbishop of Paris to have the medals struck. The apparitions were approved by the Church as authentic in 1836.

Access: Road: Located at the end of an obscure passage, off the busy one-way rue du Bac. These grounds have been trod by approximately 3000 pilgrims daily who come here for prayer and reflection.

Church of St. Joseph of the Carmes
70, rue de Vaugirard
75006 Paris
Roman Catholic Carmelite

Open To: Pilgrims, visitors coming here to pray. Open for
visits Saturdays at 15:00. Public welcome for church services.

Guests Admitted To: Church (1625), the first in Paris
dedicated to St. Joseph. Garden. Crypt.

Of Interest: During the French Revolution, one hundred and
ten victims, including three bishops, priests, monks and one
layman, were held prisoner in the nave of this church, and
slaughtered on September 2, 1792 at the foot of the stairs in the
convent garden. The martyrs were beatified in 1926.

Centre Interculturel de Bevoye
Chemin de Basse-Bevoye
57245 Peltre
Roman Catholic, Lutheran, and Reformed Church of
        Alsace-Lorraine

Tel: 87 74 56 76
Fax: 87 74 96 70
Contact: Secretary

Open To: Youth groups and other groups.

Accommodation: Hospitality is provided in the Centre for a
max. of 40 persons. Conference room, meeting rooms, games
room, relaxation room, dining room.

Guests Admitted To: Church (adjacent to the Centre.)
Grounds.

Of Interest: The Intercultural Center of Bevoye was founded
for the Catholic Dioceses of Metz, Trier, Namur, and
Luxembourg, and two Protestant churches. Young people live
and work in community, and exchange ideas of their diverse
cultures. This is done in a spirit of peace and harmony, with
renewed hope for the Europe of the future. The Center is
located at the doorway to Metz, France in central Europe at the
border junction of four countries. It is situated on an *18th c.*

farm, and the house has been remodeled since 1988 by the young people who come here.

Access: Rail: Metz Sta., then by car or bus to Peltre.

Abbaye Notre-Dame-du-Gard
Crouy-Saint-Pierre
80310 Picquigny
Roman Catholic Freres Auxiliares

Tel: 03 22 51 40 50
Fax: 03 22 51 24 79
Contact: Le Gard Accueil

Open To: Individuals, families, groups for Retreats, Seminars, Conferences, Meetings of a religious, cultural, agricultural, or tourist nature for a time of silence, rest and renewal.

Accommodation: Hospitality is provided in the center's guest rooms. Meals available.

Guests Admitted To: Abbey Church to join the congregation for liturgical services. Grounds.

Of Interest: Abbaye Notre-Dame-du-Gard was originally founded by the Congregation of Citeaux in 1137. St. Bernard, the Father of the Cistercian Order, entered monastic life here in 1112. At the time of his death in 1153 he had founded three hundred and forty three Cistercian monasteries. In 1967, after sixty one years of neglect and abandonment, the Freres Auxiliares, under the leadership of their founder Fr. Paul Dentin, took possession of the ancient abbey and began restoration of the Renaissance buildings. The abbey, situated in natural wooded surroundings in the Somme Valley, is the only abbey in Somme to be re-founded as a house of spirituality, in keeping with its original founders' vocation. The priests and brothers are engaged in pastoral work, maintenance work, gardening, bee keeping, and sell honey at the abbey.

Access: Road: N35 from Amiens, 18 km. D49 from Doullens. D936 and D3 from Airaines. D10 and N1 from S'Riquier. Located between Picquigny and Amiens.

Monastere des Dominicaines
Notre-Dame de Beaufort
35540 Plerguer
Roman Catholic

Tel: 02 99 48 07 57
Fax: 02 99 48 48 95
Contact: Soeur Hoteliere

Open To: Individuals, groups, married couples, pilgrims, retreatants seeking a time apart in a monastic atmosphere of silence and peace for spiritual renewal. Possibility to meet with one of the sisters.

Accommodation: Hospitality is provided in the Hotellerie in 15 one or two-bedded rooms. Conference rooms. Max. stay 10 days. Arrangements to be made at least a week in advance.

Guests Admitted To: Chapel *(18th c.)* to join the sisters for Mass and the Divine Office, sung in French. All are welcome. Gift Shop.

Of Interest: The Monastery of Our Lady of Beaufort *(16th c. Chateau de Beaufort)*, a Breton manor, is situated in the center of a forest bordering a small lake. These Dominican Sisters have resided here since 1963, when they began restoration work, with the help of benefactors, on the buildings that had been abandoned for eighteen years. They were able to recapture the authentic character of the buildings. Some of the sisters are artisans, creating products such as candles, liturgical ornaments, dyed fabrics, and make honey and jam.

Access: Rail: To Dol de Bretagne (Line Saint-Malo), then 8 km. by taxi. Road: N137 (Rennes-Saint Malo), Exit Plerguer-Vieux-Bourg in direction of Dol. Monastery 3 km.

Abbaye Sainte-Anne de Kergonan
B. P. 11
56340 Plouharnel
Roman Catholic Benedictine

Tel: 33 97 52 30 75
Contact: Father in Charge

Open To: Individuals, groups (men and youths) for Retreats. Spiritual Direction available. Day visitors welcome from 11:00 – 12:30 and 14:00 – 18:00.

Accommodation: Hospitality is provided in the Guest House in several single bedrooms.

Guests Admitted To: Abbey Church (1975) to join the monks for liturgical services. Principal Feast Days: July 11 – St. Benedict; July 26 – St. Anne; Aug. 16 – St. Armel; Oct. 4 – Consecration. Gift Shop. Grounds.

Of Interest: Abbaye Sainte-Anne de Kergonan was founded in 1897 from Solesmes Abbey. The town of Auray, famous for the Church of Sainte-Anne d'Auray, is a pilgrim resort. The abbey is situated near the sea on the Brittany Peninsula.

Access: Rail: Paris-Quimper High Speed Train (TGV) Line and Lyon-Quimper and Bordeaux-Quimper Lines to Auray Sta. Summer: Auray-Quiberon Line to Plouharnel-Carnac Sta., then by taxi or bus. Road: RD168 between Auray-Quiberon, less than 1 km. from Plouharnel. D768 Auray to Plouharnel. N165 – E60 Vannes to Auray.

Foyer de Charite 'La Part-Dieu'
108, rue de Villiers
78300 Poissy
Roman Catholic

Tel: 01 39 65 12 00
Fax: 01 30 74 71 65
Contact: Secretary

Open To: Individuals, groups for Retreats in an oasis of peace, silence, space and beauty. A knowledge of French is suggested. There is a choice of a Five-Day Retreat or twenty-four hour Weekend Recollections.

Accommodation: Hospitality is provided in the Retreat House in 90 single, 25 double bedrooms. Bathrooms each floor.

Guests Admitted To: Chapel. Grounds.

Of Interest: In 1936 the first foyer was founded in Chateauneuf de Galaure, according to the spiritual discernment of Marthe Robin in collaboration with Fr. Finet. Some retreats are preached in English at this original foyer. The primary mission of over seventy foyers worldwide is to conduct retreats.

The Foyers of Charity are Catholic communities of consecrated laymen and women, headed by a priest, the Father of the Foyer, who follow the example of the early Christians. They live a life of prayer, and work in the world as witnesses to the teachings of Jesus Christ, in a spirit of faith, hope and charity.

Access: Rail: Sta. Poissy 3 km. Road: A13 – A14, Exit Poissy. Paris 17.6 km.

Monastere de Sainte-Claire   Tel: 03 84 37 11 40
13, rue Sainte-Colette   Fax: 03 84 37 07 53
39800 Poligny   Contact: Guest Sister
Roman Catholic, Franciscan Order of St. Clare

Open To: Pilgrims, individuals for Retreats, or simply a time apart in a spiritual setting. Easter to October.

Accommodation: Hospitality is provided for retreatants in 4 rooms. The Hostel, one large room, is available to those with sleeping bags, who come for a time of prayer.

Guests Admitted To: Chapel to join the nuns for liturgical services, sung in French. Shrine of St. Colette (reliquary with the saint's relics). Feast Day: March 6. Video of her life. Monastic Boutique.

Of Interest: The Monastery of St. Clare in Poligny was founded by St. Colette in 1415. While residing here for ten years, she founded seventeen other monasteries. St. Colette passed away at the Monastery of Gand in Belgium in 1447. Her sacred remains were brought to Poligny in 1783. The nuns were forced to abandon the monastery during the French Revolution, but returned in 1817. There are many beautiful works of art in the chapel, and the reliquary is considered a masterpiece, done in precious metals. Nearby is the Collegial Saint-Hippolyte with its beautiful collection of statues from the Burgundian School.

Access: Air: Nearest Airports Lyons –Satolas and Geneve-Cointrin, then 1 ½ h. by road. Rail: SNCF: Poligny Sta., then a 20 min. walk. TGV from Paris, 2 ½ h. Connections from major cities and Belgium, Switzerland, Italy, Germany, Great Britain.

Fraternite de la Vierge des Pauvres
540, chemin de Bourricos
40200 Pontenx-Les-Forges
Roman Catholic Benedictine

Tel/Fax: 05 58 07 45 22
Contact: Guest Brother

Open To: Individuals, groups for Retreats. Church visitors are required to dress appropriately. An atmosphere of silence and prayer must be observed. There is the possibility of sharing in the prayer life of the brothers, their work, and meals.

Accommodation: Hospitality is provided in the guest quarters in 3 four-bedded rooms, shared bathrooms. Also, the community offers simple, self-catering accommodation 1.7 km. from the monastery in The Pavilion, 15 beds. Two kitchens, bathrooms, chapel. Supervised by a sister.

Guests Admitted To: St.-Jean-de-Bourricos Chapel *(11th c.).* The Fountain on monastery grounds.

Of Interest: The small Community of Brothers of the Fraternity of the Virgin of the Poor was founded in 1956, inspired by the spirituality of Charles de Foucauld. This small rural monastery, dedicated to the Virgin of Banneux, is situated in the center of the Landes Forest in a deserted village. A beautiful Roman chapel is at the heart of the complex, reflecting the peace and simplicity of the site.

Access: Rail: SNCF: To Labouheyre. Road: Coming north from Bordeaux or south from Bayonne, take RN10 to Labouheyre, Exit 16. Take D626 in direction of Mimizan. After 13 km., turn left and follow signs for the 'Chapelle de Bourricos.'

Les Rendez-Vous de Pontigny   Tel: 86 47 47 17
17, rue de l'Abbe Tauleigne – Cidex 51 Fax: 86 47 42 21
89230 Pontigny   Contact: Secretary
Maison de la Mission de France

Open To: Individuals, groups, families, youths for educational and cultural programs. Year round.

Accommodation: Hospitality is provided in the Guest House in bedrooms and a mini-dormitory (max. 30 persons.) Dining room, kitchen, conference rooms. Also, large camping area within a park.

Guests Admitted To: Grounds, including theater area.

Of Interest: The village of Pontigny is located in the center of Champagne and Bourgogne between Auxerre and Troyes in the Serein Valley. It offers a peaceful, relaxing environment in natural surroundings, with pleasant walks to the village and in the forest. The famous Chablis Vineyard is ten kilometers away, and the monumental Cistercian Abbey of France is a few minutes walk from the house. Auxerre, twenty kilometers northeast of Pontigny, is a city of historic art, and visitors will also enjoy the picturesque medieval village of Noyers.

Access: Rail: Sta. Laroche Migennes or Sta. St. Florentin-Vergigny. Road: A6 from Paris, Exit Auxerre North on N77 in direction of Troyes. A5 from Melun. A6 from Lyon, Exit Nitry in direction Tonnerre Chablis, then Ligny le Chatel.

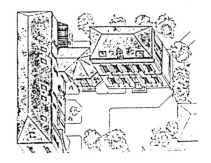

Abbaye d'Oelenberg   Tel: 03 89 81 91 23
68950 Reiningue   Contact: Father Abbot
Roman Catholic Cistercian

Open To: Pilgrims, individuals, groups for Retreats. Spiritual Direction available.

Accommodation: Hospitality is provided in 27 guest rooms.

Guests Admitted To: Abbey Church to join the monks for Mass, in Gregorian Chant, and the Divine Office in French. Grounds.

Of Interest: Abbaye d'Oelenberg was founded in 1046 by the Regular Canons of St. Augustine. Over the centuries, monastic life declined as a result of wars and conflicts. From 1626 to 1773 the Jesuit Fathers of Fribourg-en-Brisgau brought a renewal of spiritual life to the monastery; however, the French Revolution ended it all, and the state took over the property. In 1825 Trappist monks from Darfeld established a foundation here, and their religious fervor has been constant despite many hardships resulting from WWI and WWII. The abbey is situated on park-like grounds and farmland. The monks sell wheat flour, eggs, and vegetables as well as products from other monasteries.

Access: Air: Airport Mulhouse-Bale 30 km. Rail: SNCF: Sta. Mulhouse, then by bus 'Chopin,' Line Reiningue-Thann. Road: D20, 22 km. west of Mulhouse. A36, Exit Thann.

Monastere du Broussey   Tel: 05 56 62 60 90
33410 Rions   Fax: 05 56 62 60 79
Roman Catholic Carmelite   Contact: Le Frere Hotelier

Open To: Individuals, groups for Spiritual Retreats. Spiritual Direction available. Reservations required/stamped s.a.e.

Accommodation: Hospitality is provided in the Hotellerie in 20 bedrooms. Meals taken in silence in the dining room. Max. stay 8 days. The Sisters of Notre-Dame of Bethlehem assist with hospitality services.

Guests Admitted To: Monastery Church to join the monks for liturgical services. Chapel *(19th c.)* Library. Grounds

Of Interest: Monastere du Broussey was founded by Fr. Dominique of St. Joseph who had been chaplain to Don Carlos of Spain, was exiled to Bordeaux, and eventually went to America. The Prioress of the Carmelite Convent of Bordeaux urged him to return to Bordeaux and establish a mens' monastery. On Holy Thursday, 1841, he transferred his community to the present site. The monastery is situated among rolling hills, overlooking the Sauterne Plain on the right bank of the Garonne River, with a lovely view of the Landes Mountains. There are trails through the vineyard and woods far removed from city noise.

Access: Rail: To Cerons, then take bus coming from Bordeaux, Exit Rions. Pickup possible at bus sta. by prior arrangement. Road: A62, Exit Podensac in direction of Cadillac. Turn left at the first light in Beguey, in direction of Cardan for 3 km., then right and follow signs for the monastery.

Maison D'Accueil   Tel: 02 35 20 42 57
14, rue du Pere Arson   Contact: Secretary
76700 Rogerville
Roman Catholic, La Fraternite du Pere Arson

Open To: Individuals, groups for Retreats, Meetings, Seminars and Holidays.

Accommodation: Hospitality is provided in the House of Prayer in 18 single and double bedrooms. Showers and bathrooms each floor. Conference rooms.

Guests Admitted To: House chapel. Grounds.

Of Interest: The Fraternity – the Auxiliary Sisters of St. Francis of Assisi and the Auxiliary Brothers – was founded by Fr. Arson (1874 – 1948.) They collaborate in the management and programs of the house. Maison D'Accueil is situated close to the village facing the Normandy Bridge within close proximity to celebrated abbeys of Normandy.

Access: Road: A131 from Tancarville or Le Havre, Exit Rogerville. A29 from Normandy Bridge. N15 from Yvetot in direction of Le Havre, Exit Harfleur, direction Gonfreville and Rogerville.

Foyer de Charite 'Maria Mater'
B. P. 17
06330 Roquefort Les Pins
Roman Catholic

Tel: 04 92 60 30 00
Fax: 04 92 60 30 01
Contact: Secretary

Open To: Individuals, groups, 18 years of age and up, for Five-Day Retreats in silence. Child care available. Groups may bring their own leader. Booking form sent on request.

Accommodation: Hospitality is provided in the Retreat House.

Guests Admitted To: Chapel. Grounds.

Of Interest: The retreats promote the Gospel message of Jesus Christ, and also give special honor to Mary, Mother of Our Lord. This foyer is situated in a large park near the Mediterranean Alps, an area with a mild and pleasant climate.

Access: Air: Nice Airport is the closest. Rail: Sta. Cagnes sur Mer, then by car, stop at Roquefort 'Le Colombier.'

Abbaye Notre-Dame de Randol
63450 Saint-Amant-Tallende
Roman Catholic Benedictine

Tel: 0473 39 31 00
Contact: Guestmaster

Open To: Men for Retreats. Spiritual Direction available.
Public welcome for church services.

Accommodation: Hospitality is provided in the monastery's
guest quarters. Meals taken with the monks in the refectory.
Self-catering guest houses are available in the nearby hamlet of
Randol to accommodate women and married couples.

Guests Admitted To: Abbey Church to join the monks for
liturgical services. Grounds that are open to guests.

Of Interest: Abbaye Notre-Dame de Randol was founded in
1968. It is situated amidst magnificent scenery on the side of a
mountain. The monks broadcast the Mass with Gregorian
Chant daily on the radio to different regions of France.

Access: Road: N9 from Montpelier, exit in direction of
Champeix. Take D28 to D719 before St.-Saturnin. Follow signs
to the abbey. Or N9 from Riom, exit in direction of St.-Saturnin
and St.-Amant-Tallende. Take left onto D28 and right onto
D719. Or, Motorway Clermont – FD – Montpelier, Exit North 5,
then 6 km. via St.-Saturnin.

Abbaye de Fleury
45730 Saint-Benoit-sur-Loire
Roman Catholic Benedictine

Tel: 02 38 35 72 43
Fax: 02 38 35 77 71
Contact: Frere Hotelier

Open To: Individuals, groups for Retreats for a few days.
Spiritual Direction available. Book by letter only. Pilgrimage
groups write to Brother in Charge of Visitors to make arrange-
Ments to visit the basilica.

Accommodation: Hospitality is provided for retreatants in the
Hotellerie. Two hotels, restaurants, and B&B in the village.

Guests Admitted To: Abbey Basilica to join the monks for liturgical services. Crypt (reliquary with the relics of St. Benedict.) Abbey library.

Of Interest: Abbaye de Fleury was founded in the 7th c. It is situated on the north shore of the Loire River. In 1944 the abbey was restored by the monks of the Abbey of Pierre-qui-Vire. The monks live a life of silence and prayer. Some of them are artists and craftsmen, creating enamel products, porcelain painting, and they make candles and candies, for sale in the library to the right of the basilica.

Access: Rail: SNCF: Paris (Austerlitz Sta.) to Orleans, then rapid transit Du Val De Loire. At train sta., take rapid transit Line 3. Road: Orleans 35 km.

Monastere N.-D. des Petites Roches   Tel: 04 76 08 31 13
38660 Saint-Bernard du Touvet   Fax: 04 76 08 32 17
Roman Catholic   Contact: Guest Sister
Cisterciennes Bernardines D'Esquermes

Open To: Individuals, groups for Retreats, or simply for a time apart for prayer and spiritual renewal. Spiritual Direction available. English spoken. Guests are asked to respect the quiet of the house, especially during evening and early morning.

Accommodation: Hospitality is provided in 20 rooms (approx. 40 beds), and in 3 ten-bedded dormitories. Bathrooms each floor. Conference rooms. Max. stay 15 days.

Guests Admitted To: Chapel to join the nuns for services.

Of Interest: Monastere Notre-Dame des Petites Roches was built in 1987, and is located in a small village beneath the massive foothills of the Chartreuse Mountains facing the Belledonne Range.

Access: Air: Satolas-Lyon Airport, then 100 km. by car. Rail: From Grenoble, then 30 km. from station. Taxi service Eyraud. Road: N90 and A41.

Maison Ker-Avinou
Monastere des Augustines
62, rue de Vannes
56400 Sainte-Anne D'Auray
Roman Catholic Augustinian Sisters

Tel: 02 97 57 51 91
Contact: Guest Sister

Open To: Individuals, small groups who desire a time of rest, relaxation and silence in a prayerful environment.

Accommodation: Hospitality is provided in the Guest House in 14 single rooms with shower rooms. Relaxation room with TV, games. Library. Max. stay one month.

Guests Admitted To: Chapel to join the sisters for Mass and the Divine Office.

Of Interest: The Basilica of Sainte-Anne D'Auray is one of the most popular pilgrimage centers in France. St. Anne, mother of the Blessed Virgin Mary, appeared at this site in 1625 with the message that our Lord wished her to be honored here. The Augustine Monastery and Guest House are situated in a peaceful, verdant landscape close to the basilica and other centers of pilgrimage.

Access: Rail: Auray Sta., Paris- Quimper Line, then 6.4 km. by taxi. Road: Paris – Rennes – Vannes – Sainte-Anne D'Auray or Paris – Nantes – Vannes – Sainte-Anne D'Auray.

Association Culturelle de Pommiers
Ancien Prieure Benedictin
6, rue General-Leclerc
42100 Saint-Etienne

Tel: 04 77 65 44 88
Fax: 04 77 65 56 63
Contact: President

Open To: Students on Holiday. Day visitors.

Accommodation: Hospitality is provided in 18 rooms. Restaurant/bar, snack bar, grocery store. Campground with snack bar.

Guests Admitted To: Diocesan Church (*11ᵗʰ* c. Priory Church) for services.

Of Interest: A Benedictine Priory was founded here in the *9ᵗʰ* c. and had close ties to the monasteries of Nantua and Cluny. With the assistance of the villagers, the monks labored to turn primitive land into productive agricultural fields. In the *14ᵗʰ* c. the populace of Pommiers built fortified walls to protect themselves from brigands. After the *18ᵗʰ* c. the priory was sold. The last owner was a religious man who opened a retreat house for priests on the premises. The complex is presently owned by the General Council of Loire. It is situated along the banks of the Aix River in the ancient village of Pommiers-en-Forez, which dates back to the Bronze Age.

Access: Road: A72, Exit St.-Germain-Laval. Feurs 20 km. Roanne 35 km. Saint-Etienne 60 km. Clermont-Ferrand 90 km. Lyon 110 km.

Hotellerie Notre-Dame du Laus
05130 Saint-Etienne-Le-Laus
Roman Catholic

Tel: 04 92 50 30 73
Fax: 04 92 50 90 77
Contact: Rector

Open To: Pilgrims, individuals, groups, families for Retreats, Conferences, Meetings, and other spiritual activities.

Accommodation: Hospitality is provided in the Hotellerie in simple, family-style rooms. Sitting rooms, TV, library, kinder-garden. Also, self-catering dormitory and campgrounds.

Guests Admitted To: Basilica of Notre-Dame du Laus (1669), with original Chapel 'Bon Rencontre' within the sanctuary church. Grounds.

Of Interest: Sanctuaire Notre-Dame du Laus dates back to 1664 when a seventeen year old shepherdess, Benoite Rencurel, experienced the first of several apparitions of a beautiful lady holding a child by the hand. The Blessed Mother finally instructed Benoite to seek and find a chapel in Le Laus where they would meet daily. The sanctuary is situated in this modest mountain village, surrounded by the southern Alps.

Access: Road: 20 km. from Gap. N94 from Gap in direction of Charges. Take a right onto D942 to the sanctuary. From Marseille, RN85, Exit D942, then follow signs.

Monastere du Carmel
7, Montee des Roches
15100 Saint-Flour
Roman Catholic Carmelite

Tel: 04 71 60 01 66
Fax: 04 71 60 93 94
Contact: Mere Prieure

Open To: Women for Silent Retreats. Chapel open to all.

Accommodation: Hospitality is provided in the monastery's guest quarters for a few retreatants.

Guests Admitted To: Chapel to join the nuns for Mass and the Liturgy of the Hours, in French.

Of Interest: Carmel of Saint-Flour, founded in 1839, is situated in the Auvergne Mountains. The nuns live a life of prayer in silence and solitude. To help support their cloister, they do sewing, bind books, and make pictures for children's rooms. Their products are sold at the monastery and other centers.

Access: Rail: SNCF: St.-Flour Sta., Line Paris-Beziers, then by taxi. Road: A75.

Abbaye de Rhuys
Centre Culturel et Spirituel
Place Mgr. Ropert
56730 Saint-Gildas de Rhuys
Roman Catholic
Congregation of the Sisters of Charity of St. Louis

Tel: 97 45 23 10
Fax: 97 45 10 32
Contact: Secretary

Open To: Individuals, groups for spiritual and cultural purposes, and for rest and renewal. Reservations required months in advance.

Accommodation: Hospitality is provided in the Hotellerie in 65 bedrooms, single and double, 11 en-suite. Conference rooms, dining room, library.

Guests Admitted To: Abbey Church of St. Gildas (*11th-12th c.*). Parish Church, adjacent to the abbey.

Of Interest: Abbaye de Rhuys was rebuilt in the *16th-17th c.*, and purchased in 1825 by Madame Mole, the foundress of the congregation. The abbey is surrounded by a large garden and prairie, with access to the pristine beach by private trails. It is located two hundred meters from the sea and within close proximity to shops and other services. The small village owes its origins to the *6th c.* monastery founded by St. Gildas, who was born in Scotland. He spent his last years in Brittany, living as a hermit on an island in Morbihan Bay near Rhuys.

Access: Rail: To Vannes, 32 km. Pickup can be arranged with prior notice. Road: Nantes/Quimper – Rennes/Vannes, Exit Sarzeau.

L'Abbaye Saint-Jacut-de-la-Mer
B. P. 1
22750 Saint-Jacut-de-la-Mer
Roman Catholic Soeurs de l'Immaculee, St.-Meen-le-Grand

Tel: 96 27 71 19
Fax: 96 27 79 45
Contact: La Directrice

Open To: Individuals, groups, families, children's groups (supervised) for Retreats, Meetings, Conferences, rest and relaxation. In July – August, the house becomes a pensionne for families. Priests and religious who are convalescing are welcomed year-round. Senior citizens may enjoy extended stays during winter. Advance reservations required.

Accommodation: Hospitality is provided in the Hotellerie in 90 bedrooms with showers and bathrooms. Oratory, dining rooms, small group rooms, TV rooms, library.

Guests Admitted To: Chapel. Crypt. Grounds (garden, tennis).

Of Interest: L'Abbaye St.-Jacut-de-la-Mer was originally founded around 465 by St. Jacut. It was an influential Benedictine center of spirituality for centuries up to the French Revolution. In 1875 the Sisters of the Immaculate, St. Meen-le-Grand purchased the property that they operate as a house of hospitality and prayer.

Access: Air: Pleurtuit-Dinard 12 km. Rail: Sta. St.-Malo 20 km., Line Paris – Rennes – St.-Malo, then by bus or taxi. Sta. Plancoet 11 km., Line Paris – Lamballe – Plancoet.

Couvent de la Divine Providence   Tel: 03 87 03 00 50
57930 Saint-Jean-de-Bassel   Fax: 03 87 03 00 51
Roman Catholic   Contact: Directress
Congregation of the Sisters of Divine Providence

Open To: Individuals, groups for Retreats, Conferences, Meetings, and for those seeking a time apart in a calm, Christian atmosphere for rest and reflection. French, German and English spoken.

Accommodation: Hospitality is provided in guest houses in 45 single rooms, 5 with baths, 10 double, and 8 family bedrooms. Showers each floor. Three conference rooms, 8 meeting rooms, dining room, library.

Guests Admitted To: Chapel. Grounds. Village Church of St. John the Baptist, adjacent to the complex.

Of Interest: In 1827 the Sisters of Divine Providence purchased the property, part of which dates back to the *14th c.* In 1864 they built La Maison Sainte-Marie and La Maison Sainte-Famille. St. Joseph Home for their elderly and sick sisters is closeby, and laity are welcome to stay there as room permits. The convent is situated in the center of the village, surrounded by a park and gardens.

Access: Air: Strasbourg-Entzheim Airport 70 km. Rail: Sta. Sarrebourg and Reding 12 km., then by car or taxi, or guests may be picked up at station by house staff with prior notice. Road: A4, N4, D43, D95.

Atelier Saint-Jean Damascene
La Prade
26190 Saint-Jean-En-Royans
Parc du Vercors
Greek Orthodox

Tel: 04 75 48 66 75
Fax: 04 75 47 70 77
Contact: Director

Open To: Individuals, groups of all ages who are interested in entering the spiritual journey of painting icons as well as writing on the icons. Courses in icon painting, mosaics, frescoes, and restoration. Booking by letter only. Closed in October. Italian, French, Greek, Russian, English spoken.

Accommodation: Hospitality is provided in the Center of Sacred Art in 4 double rooms. Sanitary facilities each floor. Three workshops. Self-catering kitchen available. Max. stay 2 days to a week. Lodging, camping, restaurants available in the village.

Guests Admitted To: Chapel. Grounds.

Of Interest: The Greek Orthodox Workshop of Sacred Art, established twenty five years ago, is a branch of the Ecumenical Patriarcate of Constantinople. It is situated on park-like grounds in an isolated area close to the coast in the Drome Department of northwest France. There is a swimming pool within one kilometer and many places of interest in the area such as the Grotto of Chorange, the Abbey of St. Anthony, and other monasteries and churches.

Access: Air: Lyon-Satolas Airport 100 km. Rail: Sta.
St. Hilaire/St. Nazaire, then 10 km. by taxi. Road: D131 to
St.-Jean-En-Royans, in direction of Bouvante.

L'Abbaye Notre-Dame des Neiges   Tel: 04 66 46 50 12
07590 Saint-Laurent-les-Bains   Contact: Pere Hotelier
Roman Catholic Cistercian

Open To: Individuals, groups (usually with leader) for Retreats, for those seeking the peace and silence of a monastic setting. Monks available to assist individual retreatants.

Accommodation: Hospitality is provided for retreatants in the Hotellerie in a comfortable, friendly atmosphere.

Guests Admitted To: Abbey Church to join the monks for Mass and the Divine Office (public welcome). Audio-visual presentation about monastic life. Farm and wine caves.

Of Interest: The Abbey of Our Lady of the Snow was founded in 1850, renewing the monastic tradition that was originally established in the region by the Cistercian Abbey of Mazan in 1119. The abbey is situated on the verdant, wooded plateau of the mountains of Vivarais. In 1890 Charles de Foucauld came to the monastery and became a monk. He felt called to live the life of a hermit in North Africa, and eventually aspired to the priesthood, saying his first Mass here in 1901. He ministered to the nomads and French soldiers in Morocco where he met a martyr's death.

The monks work on their farm and in the vineyards and have produced high quality liturgical and table wines, for sale at the wine cave and by correspondence. There are popular thermal baths in the commune nearby.

Access: Rail: Sta. Bastide- St.-Laurent-les-Bains, Line Paris – Clermont-Ferrand – Nimes, then 3 km. to the abbey. Road: N88, N102, N106, Paris – Vichy – LePuy – Nimes. Mende 53 km. LePuy 65 km. Ales 84 km.

L'Abbaye Sainte-Marie de la Pierre-Qui-Vire
89630 Saint-Leger Vauban   Tel: 86 33 19 28
Roman Catholic Benedictine   Fax: 86 32 22 33
Congregation of Subiaco   Contact: Guestmaster

Open To: Pilgrims, individuals, groups, married couples who are seeking to deepen their spiritual life. Day visitors as well as residential guests.

Accommodation: Hospitality is provided in the Hotellerie for persons who are on a 'spiritual journey.' Meals served for residential guests only.

Guests Admitted To: Abbey Church to join the monks for liturgical services, sung in French, some in Gregorian Chant. Film about life at the monastery. Library. Shops.

Of Interest: L'Abbaye Ste.-Marie de la Pierre-Qui-Vire was founded in 1850. This place of silence and solitude is located in the center of the Morvan, a beautiful, rugged land of forests and granite, waterfalls and lakes. The monks live a life of prayer and are engaged in various works including hospitality, creation of books on art, production of C.D.'s and video tapes, handmade pottery, and they make cheese.

Access: Road: National 6, turn at Rouvray, then D4 in direction of St. Leger Vauban. By A6 coming from the north, exit at Avallon toward Dijon-Lyon to Rouvray. From the south, exit at Bierre-les-Semur. After RN70, head toward Precy to Rouvray, then to St. Leger Vauban. Avallon 26 km.

Monastere Saint-Elie
5, rue du Floquet
21500 Saint-Remy
Byzantine Rite Catholic, Carmelite

Tel: 03 80 92 07 40
Fax: 03 80 92 48 79
Contact: Guest Sister

Open To: Individuals, small groups for Silent Retreats.
Ecumenical.

Accommodation: Hospitality is provided in a few monastery
guest rooms.

Guests Admitted To: Chapel to join the nuns for liturgical
services in French.

Of Interest: The Carmelite Monastery of St.-Elie was founded
in 1974 by Carmel of Nancey. It is established according to the
Catholic Byzantine Rite, with a strong ecumenical spirit. The
monastery is close to Paris where there is a Byzantine Church.
Woven into their daily rhythm of prayer are works that help
support the community such as icon painting, wood icon
reproductions, oriental rosaries, and book binding. The
monastery is situated near the village church of St.-Remy.

Access: Rail: SNCF: Montbard Sta., Line Paris-Lyon, then
4 km. by taxi.

Carmel du Christ-Roi
10, Allee du Carmel
40500 Saint-Sever/Adour
Roman Catholic Carmelite

Tel: 05 58 76 00 15
Fax: 05 58 76 36 75
Contact: Soeur Hoteliere

Open To: Individuals, small groups for Retreats, or simply a
time apart in a monastic setting. Spiritual Direction available.

Accommodation: Hospitality is provided in the small
Hotellerie in single and double bedrooms.

Guests Admitted To: Monastery Church to join the nuns for
Mass and the Divine Office. Grounds.

Of Interest: Carmel of Christ the King was founded in Bordeaux, France in the early part of the *20th c.* Because of anti-clerical sentiments, the nuns were exiled to Zaurauz, Spain. In 1915 a nun of German descent, Sr. Anne of Jesus from Carmel of Compiegne, joined them, as it seemed prudent to do so during WWI. The French nuns returned to France in 1917, but she stayed on in Spain and became Prioress of Carmel of Zaurauz. In 1930, due to the serious political climate in Spain, Sr. Anne of Jesus took the Spanish Carmelites to St. Sever and founded Carmel of St. Sever. The Spanish nuns returned to their homeland in 1933. The Carmelites of St. Sever live a life of prayer, and their work includes book binding, making liturgical vestments, altar cloths, religious articles, First Communion outfits, and graphics for music composers.

Access: Road: N132, 16 km. southwest of Mont-de-Marsan.

Maison Saint-Dominique
91910 Saint-Sulpice de Favieres
Roman Catholic
Dominicaines de Bethanie

Tel: 01 64 58 54 15
Fax: 01 69 94 95 64
Contact: Soeur Hoteliere

Open To: Individuals, groups seeking a quiet time apart in the country for reflection and prayer.

Accommodation: Hospitality is provided in 20 single, 5 double bedrooms. Showers each floor. Conference room, meeting rooms, dining room. Max. length of stay 2 – 3 weeks.

Guests Admitted To: Chapel. Grounds.

Of Interest: The Congregation of Dominicans of Bethany was founded in 1864 by a young Dominican priest after preaching a retreat at a women's prison. He offered to those women who desired it the possibility of becoming nuns. They live a contemplative lifestyle that is strongly fraternal. The congregation has retreat/hospitality houses in the mountains of Switzerland overlooking Lake Sarnen, and near Rome, Italy.

Access: Rail: Sta. Breuillet-Village, then 4 km. by taxi.
Road: Paris 40 km.

Abbaye Saint-Wandrille de Fontenelle
76490 Saint-Wandrille   Tel: 02 35 96 23 11
Roman Catholic Benedictine   Fax: 02 35 56 63 41
                                    Contact: Guestmaster

Open To: Individuals, groups for Retreats. Public welcome for
Guided Tours and liturgical services.

Accommodation: Hospitality is provided for men in the
monastery in a limited number of rooms. Women, young ladies,
married couples on retreat are accommodated in St. Joseph's
Guest House.

Guests Admitted To: Abbey Church to join the monks for
liturgical services. Chapels. Grounds that are open to guests.

Of Interest: Abbaye Saint-Wandrille de Fontenelle was
founded in 649 and had a long and colorful history of spiritual
fervor that greatly contributed to religious life in France. There
were also periods of exile and hardship. In 1931 the community
returned to this ancient site which includes the 10th c. Church of
Saint-Saturnin, located on a wooded hillside, the $13^{th} - 14^{th}$ c.
ruins of the old Abbey Church, and the $17^{th} - 18^{th}$ c. conventual
buildings. The present Abbey Church was once an old barn that
was relocated in 1968 – 1969. Among their many works, the
monks reproduce documents on microfilm, and produce CD's
and cassettes of Gregorian Chant as well as organ recordings.

Access: Rail: Paris - Le-Havre Line, then 14 km. from d'Yvetot.
Road: N982.

Abbaye de Sainte-Marie-de-Boulaur
32450 Saramon   Tel: 05 62 65 40 07
Roman Catholic Cistercienne   Fax: 05 62 65 49 37
                                Contact: Soeur Hoteliere

Open To: Priests, religious, youth, groups for Retreats,
Conferences, Meetings Oct. – May. Women and families
welcome May – Sept. For those seeking a time of peace, rest
and prayer in a monastic setting.

Accommodation: Hospitality is provided in several rooms, full
board. Minimum stay 5 days.

Guests Admitted To: Abbey Church *(12th c.)* for liturgical
services. Grounds that are open to guests.

Of Interest: Abbaye de Sainte-Marie-de-Boulaur was
originally founded in 1140 by Petronille de Chemille, Abbess of
Fontevrault. The nuns live a life of prayer, study and work.
Their restoration of the ancient buildings has been under the
guidance of the Historical Society. There are frescoes in the
church from the School of Giotto *(14th c.),* and a portion of the
original church walls has been preserved. Visitors will enjoy
fresh produce and preserves from the abbey's orchard and
gardens.

Access: Rail: SNCF: Toulouse or Gimont-Cahuzae Stations,
then by taxi. Road: N124 from Toulouse, 60 km., Exit Gimont,
then 13 km. to abbey. D626 from Auch, 25 km.

Monastere de la Nativite   Tel: 03 86 65 13 41
105, rue Victor Guichard   Fax: 03 86 65 73 49
89100 Sens   Contact: Soeur Hoteliere
Roman Catholic, Les Dominicaines de l'Eucharistie

Open To: Individuals, groups for Retreats, Sessions, rest and
holidays.

Accommodation: Hospitality is provided in the Hotellerie in
single and double bedrooms (75-80 beds). Conference rooms,
meeting rooms, dining room.

Guests Admitted To: Monastery Church for Mass and the
Divine Office, sung in both French and Gregorian Chant.

Of Interest: This Institute of Contemplative Life of Dominican
Sisters of the Eucharist was founded in 1920. The monastery is
situated on park-like grounds on the outskirts of the city of
Sens, eight hundred meters from the cathedral. The sisters
share a life of prayer and work. Their chocolates are sold in the
monastery and by correspondence. Homemade jams and cakes
are sold only at the monastery.

Access: Rail: Sens Sta., then 2 km. by car or taxi.

Le Couvent Notre-Dame des Monts   Tel: 04 50 47 20 17
74310 Servoz   Contact: Guest Sister
Roman Catholic, Les Dominicaines de l'Eucharistie

Open To: Individuals, families, groups for Retreats, Sessions,
rest and holidays.

Accommodation: Hospitality is provided in the Guest House in 21 bedrooms. Small dining room, conference room, library.

Guests Admitted To: Chapel.

Of Interest: The convent and guest house are located in the Haute-Savoie Department of eastern France in the beautiful Valley of Chamonix, noted for winter sports and mountain climbing. There are wonderful views of Mont Blanc and surrounding glacial peaks. The sisters' motherhouse, the Monastery of the Nativity, is at Sens.

Access: There are coach and rail services to Servoz and the Valley of Chamonix.

Abbaye Sainte-Lioba
Quartier Saint-Germain
13109 Simiane-Collongue
Roman Catholic Benedictine

Tel: 33 4 42 22 60 60
Fax: 33 4 42 22 79 50
Contact: Guestmistress

Open To: Individuals, small groups for Retreats in an atmosphere of peace, solitude, silence and prayer. Spiritual Direction available.

Accommodation: Hospitality is provided in the monastery's guest quarters.

Guests Admitted To: Abbey Church for Mass and the Divine Office. Visitors are welcome for liturgical services.

Of Interest: Abbaye Ste.-Lioba was founded in 1966. The nuns live a life of prayer, interwoven with work, such as making liturgical vestments, pottery, and weaving.

Access: Air: Marseille-Provence Airport 20 km. Rail: Sta. Simiane-Collongue 3 km. Road: Marseille-Aix, Exit Gardanne.

Monastere Saint-Germain
Quartier Saint-Germain
13109 Simiane-Collongue
Roman Catholic Benedictine

Tel: 34 4 42 22 60 60
Fax: 34 4 42 22 79 50
Contact: Guestmaster

Open To: Individuals for Private Retreats, for those who desire the silence and prayer of the monastery. Spiritual Direction available. Visitors welcome for church services.

Accommodation: Hospitality is provided in the monastery's guest quarters. House chapel.

Guests Admitted To: Monastery Church to join the monks for Mass and the Divine Office. Grounds.

Of Interest: The Monastery of St. Germain was founded in 1987. Although their life of prayer is of primary importance in this place of peace and solitude, the monks perform handwork such as weaving, batik, and stained glass work.

Access: See page 107 – Abbaye Ste.-Lioba.

Abbaye Saint-Pierre
72300 Solesmes
Roman Catholic
Benedictine

Tel: 02 43 95 03 08
Fax: 02 43 95 68 79
From Abroad: 33 2 43 - - - - - - - -
E-mail:abbaye@solesmes.com
Contact: Guestmaster

Open To: Men for Private Retreat within the monastic enclosure. Young people for Retreats and other spiritual activities outside the enclosure. Public welcome to join the monks for liturgical services.

Accommodation: Hospitality is provided for men on retreat in the Abbey Guest House. The Youth Hostel is available for groups of 10 – 40 persons. Villa Sainte-Anne, a boarding house for men and women near the Abbey of Ste.-Cecile, is situated two blocks from St. Peter's Abbey, and is open April – Nov. and during the Christmas season. Tel: 02 43 95 45 05.

Guests Admitted To: Abbey Church for Mass and the Divine Office, sung in Gregorian Chant. Exposition of the Blessed Sacrament. Book Store.

Of Interest: Abbaye Saint-Pierre was founded in 1010. It has been involved in research on Gregorian Chant to incorporate its spiritual riches into the life of prayer. The abbey has produced publications and recordings on Gregorian Chant, as well as books about monasticism and papal teachings. Also of note are the sculptures in the transept of the church – the Burial of Christ *(15th c.)* and the Lady Chapel *(16th c.)*. The abbey is situated on the left bank of the Sarthe River. The main entrance is in the town near the Parish Church.

Access: Rail: SNCF: Paris-Nantes Line (TGV Atlantique) to Sable, then by taxi or walk to the abbey. Road: A11, Paris-Nantes, Exit Sable 3 km.

(P) Copyright Abbaye Saint-Pierre de Solesmes who have authorized publication of the information in this guide book.

Abbaye Saint-Eloi
87110 Solignac
Roman Catholic
Community du Verbe de vie

Tel: 05 55 00 50 29
Fax: 05 55 00 50 73
Contact: Retreat
Secretary

Open To: Individuals, groups for Retreats, Courses at l'Ecole de Vie Spirituelle. Also, a one year Sabbatical available. Further information sent upon request.

Accommodation: Hospitality is provided in single, double and three-bedded rooms, or in local hotels.

Guests Admitted To: Chapel. Grounds.

Of Interest: L'Ecole de Vie Spirituelle is one of the five Catholic schools of spirituality staffed by the Community du Verbe de Vie, a new community within the Catholic Church whose members include celibate persons, families, religious and priests.

Access: Rail: Limoges Sta., then Line Limoges-Brive by Uzerche. Take another train from Limoges-St.-Germain-les-Belles. Road: From Paris, N20 in direction of Toulouse-Brive, Exit Le Vigen-St.-Yrieix. From Perigueux, take D32 after Aixe-sur-Vienne. From Brive, Exit Le Vigen (D32), 3 km. to abbey.

Abbaye de la Trappe   Tel: 02 33 84 17 00
61380 Soligny la Trappe   Contact: Pere Hotelier
Roman Catholic Cistercian

Open To: Men for Silent Retreats. Youth groups for Spiritual Retreats. Day visitors welcome.

Accommodation: Hospitality is provided in the Guest House in 30 bedrooms. A remodeled sheep barn has self-catering facilities for youth.

Guests Admitted To: Abbey Church *(19th c.)* for Mass and the Divine Office. Visitor Center (audio-visual presentation). Gift Shop.

Of Interest: La Trappe dates back to 1122 when Rotrou III, a Count of Perche, built a boat-shaped chapel in memory of the death of his wife on the sinking of The Blanche-Nef. In 1140 Benedictine Monks from nearby Breuil-Benoit were invited to care for the chapel. Seven years later they joined the Trappist Order of Citeaux. After over a century of spiritual fervor and prosperity, La Trappe met with severe hardships from the atrocities of war, especially during the *14th – 15th c.,* when the King of France turned the property over to civilians. However, the abbey again flourished during the *17th c.* until the French Revolution. The dispersed monks settled in Switzerland in Chartreuse de la Val Sainte, to return to France in 1815 and to other countries. La Trappe is situated in Normandy near the Seine and Loire Rivers, and is surrounded by forest land.

Access: Rail: L'Aigle Sta., then by taxi 18 km. Road: From L'Aigle in direction of Mortagne. From Paris, Exit N12, past Ste.-Anne to Tourouvre. At 5 km., take D930.

Abbaye Saint-Michel-de-Frigolet
13150 Tarascon-Sur-Rhone Tel: 04 90 95 70 07
Roman Catholic Norbertines   Fax: 04 90 95 75 22
Srs. of St. Charles of Nancy   Contact: Mgr.of Hotellerie

Open To: Pilgrims, individuals, groups, families for Retreats,
Conferences, Vacations, Reunions, and cultural events. Varying
lengths of stay. Silence encouraged. Schedule of services and
festivals available on request. Groups contact abbey in advance
for tours.

Accommodation: Hospitality is provided in 35 rooms. Also,
Youth Hostel in 2 buildings (max. 150 persons). Meals in
Hotellerie Restaurant.

Guests Admitted To: St. Michael Church *(12th c.)*. Chapel of
Notre-Dame du Bon-Remede *(12th c.)*, integrated in the Basilica
of the Immaculate Conception *(19th c.)*. Gift Shop. Library.

Of Interest: Abbaye Saint-Michel-de-Frigolet is a place of
pilgrimage and prayer, rich in spiritual and architectural
history. It is located in the heart of the Montagnette hills,
between Tarascon, Graveson, and Boulbon.

Access: Rail: Tarascon Sta., then 13 km. Avignon Sta., then
17 km. Road: A7, Exit Avignon-Sud in direction of
Chateaurenard, Graveson to N570 – D970, then D81 to Frigolet.
A9, Exit Nimes, then D970. No public transport at Frigolet.

Congregation des Petites Soeurs Franciscaines de
        Thal-Marmoutier
1, rue du Couvent   Tel: 03 88 91 18 16
67440 Thal-Marmoutier   Fax: 03 88 91 35 15
Roman Catholic   Contact: Guest Sister

Open To: Individuals, groups for Retreats, rest and physical
and spiritual renewal in a wonderful environment of greenery
and prayer. Spiritual Direction possible. Annual program sent
upon request. Year round, except during January and May.
French, German and English spoken.

Accommodation: Hospitality is provided in single and double bedrooms, most with sink, shower, toilet (40 persons). Dining room, conference rooms, activity room. Reservations needed for full pension. Park for outdoor activities.

Guests Admitted To: Chapel to join the sisters for Eucharistic celebration, Lauds, Vespers, charismatic prayer. Adoration of the Blessed Sacrament on first Fridays.

Of Interest: In 1826, as a result of the French Revolution, Abbot Bruno Francois Liebermann evangelized the region, and Christians flocked to the Church of Haegen in the village of Thal. Two young women, Therese Hopfner and Rosina Morgenthaler, felt called by God to found an order of religious and sought the guidance of the abbot. Their convent began to attract other young women, and they adopted the Rule of the Third Order of St. Francis. In 1934 they were accepted into the Franciscan family. Marmoutier, with its Benedictine Abbey, dates back to the year 600. The abbey flourished during the $11^{th} - 12^{th}$ c. when the church was built. There are many places of interest in the area, and the beautiful Vosges Mountains offer opportunities for excursions through the forest.

Access: Rail: Line Strasbourg-Paris to Saverne Sta., then by taxi. Road: RN4 Strasbourg-Saverne, past Marmoutier, then in direction of Otterswiller and Thal-Marmoutier.

Monastere Sainte-Claire   Contact: Guest Sister
11 bis, avenue Roger Salengro
51430 Tinqueux
Roman Catholic Franciscan, Order of Poor Clares

Open To: Individuals, groups for Retreats and other spiritual activities.

Accommodation: Hospitality is provided in the monastery's guest quarters.

Guests Admitted To: Chapel to join the nuns for Mass and the Divine Office in French.

Of Interest: This was the first Poor Clare Monastery founded in France in 1220. Besides their life of prayer, the nuns bake wafers for Holy Communion, make liturgical vestments, paint icons, and paint on ceramics. The monastery is located in the vicinity of Reims, with easy access to that ancient city and its magnificent Cathedral of Reims *(13ᵗʰ c.)*.

Access: Rail: SNCF: Reims Sta., then to Tinqueux by bus or taxi. Road: Approx. 128 km. northeast of Paris.

Abbaye Notre-Dame d'Ubexy   Tel: 3 29 38 25 90
88130 Ubexy   Fax: 3 29 38 05 90
Roman Catholic Cistercienne   Contact: Guest Sister

Open To: Individuals, groups, youth groups for Silent Retreats. For those wishing to spend time in a monastic setting, sharing in the spiritual activities of the nuns.

Accommodation: Hospitality is provided in single and double guest rooms in the monastery, and in a six-bedded dormitory. Max. stay 2 weeks.

Guests Admitted To: Abbey Church to join the nuns for Mass and the Divine Office, chanted in French, with parts in Gregorian Chant. Artisan Shop. Book Shop.

Of Interest: Abbaye Notre-Dame d'Ubexy was founded in 1841. It is situated in Ubexy in the countryside. The nuns share a life of prayer and work, their main industry that of baking altar

Bread. They also make lace, rugs, and have an active ministry of hospitality.

Access: Rail: Line Nancy-Epinal-Remiremont. Road: N57 and D33. Charmes 6 km. Epinal 25 km.

L'Abbaye Notre-Dame de Belloc   Tel: 59 29 65 55
64240 Urt   Contact: Frere Hotelier
Roman Catholic Benedictine, Congregation of Subiaco

Open To: Men only for Retreats. Spiritual Direction available.

Accommodation: Hospitality is provided in the Abbey Guest House in 19 single, 7 double bedrooms. Sanitary facilities each floor. Conference room.

Guests Admitted To: Abbey Church to join the monks for Mass and the Diving Office in French. Once a week Mass is celebrated in the Basque language. Library.

Of Interest: L'Abbaye Notre-Dame de Belloc was founded in 1875. It is located in Basque country close to the Spanish border, and twenty kilometers from the coast. For years the monks had supported themselves through agricultural work. Today they make goat cheese, using traditional methods of local shepherds. They also weave virgin wool rugs, and manage the Library Siloe-Ezkila. There are many places of interest for excursions into both French and Spanish Basque country.

Access: Air: Biarritz Airport, then by taxi. Rail: Bayonne, then 20 km.

Abbaye Notre-Dame-du-Pre   Contact: Guest Sister
76540 Valmont
Roman Catholic Benedictine

Open To: Individuals, married couples, families for Retreats, or a peaceful time apart for rest and renewal. Spiritual Direction available. An atmosphere of silence is encouraged.

Accommodation: Hospitality is provided in the Abbey Guest House in several rooms.

Guests Admitted To: Chapel to join the sisters for liturgical services. Library. Grounds.

Of Interest: Benedictine Sisters came to Valmont from Lisieux in 1994, and they began restoration work on this ancient abbey.

Access: Rail: SNCF: To Fecamp, Rouen, or Yvetot, then by bus or taxi. Road: Autoroute de Normandie from Paris, 180 km., Exit Pont de Brotonne, in direction of Valmont.

Fraternite Monastique de Jerusalem   Tel: 03 86 32 33 61
Place de la Basilique   Fax: 03 86 33 36 93
89450 Vezelay   Contact: Frere Hotelier
Roman Catholic

Open To: Pilgrims, retreatants wishing to spend time in an atmosphere of prayer while visiting the Sanctuary of Sainte-Madeleine. Spiritual Direction available. Advance reservation.

Accommodation: Hospitality is provided in the Hotellerie 'Bethany' in 20 rooms. Also, 18 beds available in the Hotellerie 'Saint-Bernard'.

Guests Admitted To: Monastery Church to join the community for Mass and the Divine Office, sung in French to polyphonie. Adoration of the Blessed Sacrament. Grounds.

Of Interest: The Monastic Fraternity of Jerusalem was founded in 1975, and includes both nuns and monks. They share their liturgical life with the thousands of pilgrims and tourists who visit the Basilica of St. Madeleine nearby. The saint's relics are in the crypt of the basilica.

Access: Rail: Sermizelles Sta., then 10 km. Road: A6, Exit Nitry. Avallon 15 km. Paris 220 km.

Notre-Dame des Neiges
rue du Lycee Polonais
38250 Villard-de-Lans
Roman Catholic, Soeurs de La Retraite

Tel: 04 76 95 15 75
Contact: Guest Sister

Open To: Individuals, married couples, small groups, families for Retreats, Vacations, other spiritual activities, and rest.

Accommodation: Hospitality is provided in the Guest House in 35 beds, single and two-bedded rooms, some with shower and bathroom. Parking.

Guests Admitted To: Chapel. Grounds.

Of Interest: Our Lady of the Snows Guest House is situated in the center of the village, yet it offers a peaceful and quiet environment, surrounded by mountains, pastures and forests. The village has facilities for alpine skiing, ice skating, swimming, tennis, and horseback riding. For those wishing to go sightseeing, there are organized excursions.

Access: Road: N6 and A43 from Lyon to Bourgoin. N85 and A48 from Bourgoin to Voreppe, then in direction of Pont de Veurey and Villard-de-Lans. Good public transport. Grenoble 32 km.

La Chapelle Notre-Dame du Chene   Tel: 02 43 95 48 01
72300 Vion   Fax: 02 43 92 31 72
E-mail:ND.Chene@wanadoo.fr   Contact: Director
Roman Catholic Diocesan Priests (Le Mans)

Open To: Pilgrims, individuals, families, groups, including
children's groups for Two-Day Marian Retreats, Seminars,
Conferences, study time, or group may bring its own program.
Reservations required.

Accommodation: Hospitality is provided in the Spirituality
Center, and lodging is personalized according to the wishes and
requirements of the guests. Picnic lunch or meal arranged with
advance notice. A community of lay persons assist diocesan
priests in running the center.

Guests Admitted To: Basilica of Notre-Dame du Chene for
liturgical services. Diaporama. Library. Boutique. Grounds.

Of Interest: In 1494 local inhabitants noticed that a large oak
tree was always filled with doves, and there were small lights
surrounding the tree. The priest of Vion placed a small statue
of the Virgin Mary at the site, and pilgrims began to come here
to pray. The same statue is in the basilica today. A small
chapel was built in 1515 at this special place of pilgrimage.
Paintings in the basilica depict incidents relating to Marian
devotion.

Access: Road: A11, Exit N10 (Sable-Le Flece), then 7 km. on
D306. Sable 5 km. Le Mans, Laval, and Angers 50 km.

O Jesus,
Give me stillness of soul in Thee.
Let Thy mighty calmness reign in me.
Rule me, O Thou King of peace.

St. John of the Cross

St. Colette

PRAYER OF ST. COLETTE

Blessed be the Hour in which our Lord Jesus,
true God and true Man, was born.

Blessed be the Holy Spirit,
by whom He was conceived.

Blessed be the glorious Virgin Mary,
of whom this God-Man was born.

May the Lord hear our prayers
by the intercession of the glorious Virgin Mary,
and by the remembrance of the Most Sacred Hour
in which the God-Man was born,
that all the desires may be accomplished
for their glory and our salvation.

O JESUS CHRIST! Our Savior,
source of Faith and all Tenderness,
for the glory of your Name,
hear our humble prayer
and grant us what we desire for,
Your Eternal Life.

AMEN.